MANAGEMENT DIMENSIONS
OF DEVELOPMENT

Kumarian Press Library of Management for Development

New Directions
in
Development Management

Series Editor
Lawrence S. Graham
University of Texas at Austin

Managing Organizations in Developing Countries:
An Operational and Strategic Approach

Moses N. Kiggundu

MANAGEMENT DIMENSIONS OF DEVELOPMENT

PERSPECTIVES AND STRATEGIES

Milton J. Esman

Kumarian Press

Printed in the United States of America

Cover design by Laura Augustine
Edited by Linda Lotz
Proofread by Linda Hogan
Typeset by Tom Jakups

Printed with soy-based ink on acid-free paper by Edwards Brothers

Library of Congress Cataloging-in-Publication Data

Esman, Milton J. (Milton Jacob), 1918–
    Management dimensions of development : perspectives and strategies /
Milton J. Esman
        p.   cm. — (Kumarian Press library of management for
development. New directions in development management)
    Includes bibliographical references and index.
    ISBN 0-931816-65-3 (alk. paper). — ISBN 0-931816-64-5 (pbk. : alk. paper)
    1. Public administration—Developing countries. 2. Management—
Developing countries. 3. Economic development. 4. Developing countries—
Social policy. 5. Developing countries—Economic policy. I. Title. II. Series.
JF60.E73   1991
351.82'091724—dc20   91-26410

05   04   03   02   01   00   99   98   97   96   10 9 8 7 6 5 4

CONTENTS

INTRODUCTION

I WAS PRESENT AT THE CREATION OF THE FIELD OF DEVELOPMENT ADMINISTRA-tion as a serious intellectual enterprise. As a participant, observer, and contributor to this enterprise, I have been fortunate to survive, mostly intact, into its fourth decade. Yet this book is not intended as an intellectual autobiography or as a history of this enterprise. Instead, I have attempted an assessment of the state of the art in this fourth decade and some intimations of what the future may hold.

"Development administration" has evolved, for no particular reason that I can discern, into "development management," with no significant changes in substance or methodology. Although scholars who have shaped this field have striven for academic rigor, their main concerns have been normative and applied: the contribution of scholarship to improving the human condition. Their appreciation of the complexities inherent in induced societal change has inhibited the elaboration of grand theory. While the field's pioneers confronted the dilemmas of the declining colonial era with its hesitant and belated post–World War II commitment to development, the subject was transformed by the precipitous expansion of the U.S. imperium into terra incognita in Asia, Latin America, and Africa. These encounters through technical assistance with the realities of Third World governments revealed that the conceptual equipment of Western, particu-larly American, public administration was inadequate to the task at hand.

This challenge produced several early nodes of interest, activity, and publication. Among them were the Indiana University group (Riggs 1964; Siffin 1957), the Michigan State group (Weidner 1964), the Syracuse group (Gross 1964; Swerdlow 1963; Waldo 1970), the Southern California group (Sherwood and Pfiffner 1967; Gable 1959), the Harvard group (Fainsod 1963; Montgomery 1966), the Pittsburgh group (Esman 1966; Katz 1970), and individuals including Hanson (1959), Schaffer (1973), Maddick (1963),

1

Braibanti (1969), and Heady (1966). Their collective, if diffuse, efforts were focused by the Comparative Administration Group inspired by Fred Riggs (1971) and the Interuniversity Research Program on Institution Building, of which I was research director (1972b). Both of them were awarded critical financial support by the Ford Foundation through the efforts of George Gant, Clarence Thurber, and Irwin Sanders.

The founding generation included talented and creative scholars driven by the optimistic conviction that they were shaping a new and important discipline. What their early efforts lacked in rigor and coherence was more than compensated for by the variety of their approaches and the keen insights they generated and debated. Nearly all the concerns on which their successors have focused, with growing success—such as participation, decentralization, implementation, and learning approaches—were represented in these early writings even when they were not the dominating themes. Although there were many skeptics, a number of intellectual premises combined to constitute common points of departure for these early writings. These can be summarized in a few propositions:

1. Because of its pronounced technocratic orientation, mainline U.S. public administration needed strong infusions from politics and the other behavioral social sciences, which had flowered in the 1950s, if it was to become relevant to developmental needs and aspirations in rapidly changing Third World environments.

2. U.S. public administration would have to incorporate cross-cultural insights and analytic methods from such disciplines as cultural anthropology and social communications in order to adapt to the historical and institutional realities of non-Western societies.

3. Public administration is instrumental, indeed essential, to orderly social and economic development, but it must shift its emphasis from the maintenance of law, order, and managerial routines to the promotion and guidance of far-reaching societal changes.

4. Development is a universal process of modernization and capacity building; its dimensions and methods, including administrative requirements, are reasonably well understood; they can be taught, learned, and replicated with modifications from country to country.

5. Developmental change can be planned, guided, and facilitated by purposeful interventions; its principal agents should be the modernizing elites of indigenous societies, assisted and supported by experts from industrialized countries.

6. These elites should function mainly through the state, which is the macroinstitution best suited to design, lead, and manage on behalf of society the processes of social and economic development.

In the late 1970s, the second generation of scholars and writers on development administration emerged. This was important because they constituted the critical mass of young, talented, and committed minds that would ensure the continuity of this field of inquiry. This cohort, in which scholars from less developed countries are represented, includes such now familiar names as Rondinelli (1987), White (1990), Bryant (1982), Kiggundu (1989), Ingle (1979), Uphoff (1986a, 1986b), Korten (1980), Lindenberg and Crosby (1981), Chambers (1974), Brinkerhoff (1990), Leonard (1977), and Paul (1982). These names and the references cited are only examples of the prolific output that has invigorated, but also modified, the original premises that had set the original direction for scholars in this field. Their central tendency has been to endorse the first three propositions above, while fundamentally reassessing, recasting, and even rejecting the last three propositions. Specifically, they tend to be much more skeptical than their predecessors of the utility of the centralized state as the main motor of developmental change and much more sensitive to autonomous collective energies within society—to decentralized, participatory, bottom-up rather than top-down strategies and processes. They are more wary of the uncertainties and contingencies inherent in induced developmental change, respectful of indigenous values and practices, concerned with the need to adjust interventions by governments and external donors to the distinctive circumstances of specific publics, and convinced of the importance of learning as a strategy for management. A renewed emphasis on developmental ethics, especially as they affect the obligations of public managers, appears as a theme in many of their writings.

Many of their insights and contributions have been embraced with appreciation by their elders, they too having profited from experiential learning, fresh concepts, and reassessment of elements of their original paradigm. Thus the current state of the art (circa 1991), which I attempt to capture and interpret in this short book, incorporates cumulative perspectives, experiences, and reflections of members of both the founding and the successor generations. What I can claim as the distinctive message of this book is its elaboration of a pluralistic strategy for guiding social and economic development, including various patterns by which diverse actors and structures in state and society interact in pursuit of developmental goals. I emphasize, of course, the roles of public development managers in implementing pluralistic strategies, including the multiorganizational networks through which they increasingly function.

I am especially grateful to Lawrence Graham for persuading me to undertake this effort under the sponsorship of the Section on International and Comparative Administration of the American Society for Public Administration. Louise White, Wendell Schaeffer, Marcus Ingle, John Montgomery, and Coralie Bryant provided expert and thoughtful comments on an earlier draft.

1

STATE, SOCIETY, AND DEVELOPMENT

THE NOTION OF SOCIAL AND ECONOMIC DEVELOPMENT AS A CENTRAL GOAL OF public policy and of international concern emerged in the first decade after World War II as numerous former colonies, first in Asia and the Middle East, then in Africa and the Caribbean, gained political independence. For them, as for most of Latin America, political independence without steady and broadly based improvement in economic capacities and in material levels of living would be a hollow achievement. If European and North American countries could achieve high standards of material and social well-being for the great majority of their citizens, so could the later developers. The knowledge and the technologies needed to overcome poverty, ignorance, and disease and to foster economic growth were presumed to be available. What seemed to be needed to fulfill these expectations were good leadership, sound policies, high-level skills, and additional capital; generous assistance with the latter two elements would be available from such international agencies as the United Nations and the World Bank as well as from the wealthier industrialized countries. In the wake of economic development, open and democratic political and governmental institutions were expected to emerge.

Although the concept of development has been and remains imprecise, it connotes steady progress toward improvement in the human condition; reduction and eventual elimination of poverty, ignorance, and disease; and expansion of well-being and opportunity for all. It entails rapid change, but change alone is insufficient; it must be directed to specific ends. Development involves societal transformation—political, social, and cultural as well as economic; it implies modernization—secularization, industrialization, and urbanization—but not necessarily Westernization. It is multidimensional, with scholars and practitioners disagreeing, however, on relative emphasis, priority, and timing.

5

Development dimensions include:

1. *Economic growth.* The indispensable material base for a better life.

2. *Equity.* Fair distribution of the fruits of economic expansion.

3. *Capacity.* Cultivation of skills, institutions, and incentives that enable societies to sustain improvements and to cope with fresh challenges.

4. *Authenticity.* While learning from foreign experience, the distinctive qualities of each society are expressed in its institutions and practices.

5. *Empowerment.* Expanded opportunities for individuals and collectivities to participate and make their influence felt in economic and political transactions.

These concepts are sufficiently elastic that they command a near universal constituency that diverges, however, on specific applications. What has been and remains significant and distinctive to this era is that these aspirations are considered both legitimate and achievable on a universal scale, the framework for inspiring public policies both within less developed countries (LDCs) and in the major international institutions.

Originally, the scarce factors for development were considered to be capital for investment and technical skills. Only later did it become apparent that managerial capabilities and administrative institutions were also needed to guide the more productive use of physical resources and human skills. Management could make an important difference in the struggle against poverty, disease, ignorance, and backwardness. To some analysts, this became the critical factor, since competent management could not only use available resources to good advantage, but could attract additional resources as well. Managerial skills and institutions, it was believed, could be readily developed. In this optimistic era it seemed not unreasonable to expect that the interval from economic "take-off" to "self-sustained growth" could be reduced to a single generation (Rostow 1960).

COMPETING PARADIGMS:
STATES, MARKETS, AND ASSOCIATIONS

These expectations and the strategies by which policies and programs would be shaped and implemented coincided with a period of high confidence in the efficacy and the beneficence of the modern state. By expanding the American state apparatus, the Roosevelt New Deal had overcome the debilitating economic depression of the 1930s. The wartime state in Britain and in the United States had mobilized and guided the resources and energies that finally defeated the Nazis and the Japanese. The economic recovery of Western Europe and Japan and the installation of welfare states were being successfully undertaken under governmental leadership (Appleby 1945). John Maynard Keynes (1936) had shown how the state could manage a capitalist, free-enterprise, market economy in such a way as to produce sustained economic growth with full employment and price stability.

Consequently, the state could and should be the prime mover in economic development, a conviction that was shared by the leaders of the newly independent states, by international and bilateral development assistance agencies, and by the great majority of scholars and publicists who provided the intellectual underpinning for this grand development enterprise. In the prevailing model of the mixed economy, most of industry, finance, and commerce would be privately owned and operated, disciplined primarily by market processes; governments would establish the policy framework for development, enforce investment priorities, control abuses by regulation, operate major enterprises that the private sector was deemed uninterested in or unsuitable for, and provide a wide range of essential public services from education to transportation to public health, from agricultural extension and irrigation to promoting and financing small industry development (Lewis 1955). During the 1960s, the U.S. Agency for International Development as well as the World Bank required all governments that desired significant flows of economic assistance to produce comprehensive multisectoral, multiyear development plans as the governmentally sanctioned framework for both macro-level economic policies and sectoral investments, public and private.

Although they recognized that the capacities of many LDC governments and their bureaucracies to undertake the complex burdens of national economic planning and macroeconomic management as well as the delivery of a host of public services were limited and under considerable stress, they nevertheless expected that these temporary deficiencies could be overcome with appropriate technical assistance. The prevailing consensus regarded the state as the appropriate macroinstitution for guiding political and social modernization and for managing economic development (Myrdal 1957; Higgins 1959). Skeptics and dissenters were brushed aside as reactionaries or cranks. LDC governments expanded their activities to intervene not only in the details of investment and price policies, but also in the direct operation of economic and commercial enterprises in all sectors of the economy. The degree of state involvement varied, but by the late 1970s, government had become the dominant force in economic development strategy and practice.

The rapid and unexpected ascendancy of neoconservative ideology in the wake of the oil shock and the economic slowdown of the 1970s, followed by political victories in Britain and the United States in 1979 and 1980, prompted a fresh look at the state. The lenses for this reassessment reflected the deep hostility toward the state in neoconservative doctrine and their enthusiasm for private enterprise and market processes (Friedman 1963; Hayek 1990). These suspicions appeared to be amply vindicated by the economic disarray and the fiscal bankruptcy that confronted so many overextended governments of LDCs in the wake of the collapse of raw material prices and the debt crises of the early 1980s. The evidence seemed to confirm the neoconservative expectancy: massive incompetence in the state's fiscal and economic management, in the provision of public services, and in the affairs of public corporations; perverse policies that inhibited production and distorted economic incentives; widespread corruption, nepotism, political patronage, and profligate waste of resources; governments overloaded far beyond their modest financial and managerial capabilities.

   In the neoconservative world view, the overblown state, to paraphrase President Reagan, had become the problem, not the solution. Prescriptions for LDCs followed their standard formulas for industrialized states: Shrink to the minimum the role of the state in the economy, privatize and deregulate, and rely as much as possible on market incentives and market discipline. The prime mover for economic growth must be free private enterprise, not the state that was inherently inefficient, wasteful of scarce resources, vulnerable to corruption, and threatening to individual liberty, especially to freedom of enterprise. Sponsored by the Reagan and Thatcher governments, supported by the new economic giants Germany and Japan, implemented by the World Bank and the International Monetary Fund (IMF), the new orthodoxy enthroned neoclassical economics as the proper guide for growth and development. The state would henceforth be restricted to functions that could not be privatized; markets would supplant the state as the centerpiece of development strategy.

   Prior to the collapse of the state-centered paradigm, an alternative perspective arose that assigned primacy neither to states nor markets. This was the thesis of development from below; that very considerable capacity for mobilizing resources, providing needed services, and dispensing mutual self-help remained latent and untapped within society, especially in local communities (Owens and Shaw 1972). By activating these underutilized potentials, communities could be encouraged by voluntary initiative and by drawing on traditional patterns of cooperation to take greater responsibility for their own development, to build participatory institutions that would reflect the interests of their members and respond to their needs and preferences rather than to those of distant governments or profit-seeking capitalists. Through their own self-managed institutions, the people could take responsibility for their own self-reliant development along democratic lines. In contrast to top-down models in which governments or capitalist firms "deliver" development to the people, leadership and initiative would rise from the grassroots. Enthusiasm for community development—aided self-help—was an early, if naive, expression of confidence in development from below (Holdcroft 1978). Grassroots initiatives would be abetted by the innovation or rediscovery of technologies appropriate to small-scale, labor-intensive activities in resource-poor environments (Schumacher 1973).

These contrasting perspectives on development were readily reduced by some of their more zealous proponents to exclusive and dogmatic ideologies. To advocates of state-centered strategies—and this included most of the leading intellectuals and government leaders in Third World countries, Marxists and non-Marxists alike—only the state could represent all the diverse elements in society, transform them into a unified general interest, guide development in directions that were both effective and equitable, and build modern integrated national communities (Esman 1966). Unregulated markets catered to the wrong ethos, to individual egoism rather than social solidarity; they tended to benefit a small minority of self-seeking businesspeople, many of them foreigners, and to neglect or exploit the great majority of the people (Nyerere 1974). Local and voluntary associations tended to be traditional and parochial in their outlook and to be dominated all too often by entrenched, reactionary, self-seeking elites.

In the opposite camp, proponents of market-based strategies argued that competitive profit seeking provided the only effective incentive for economic efficiency and economic growth that, in the long run, would benefit all members of society. Competitive discipline in free markets was the most reliable regulator of economic abuses. Government interference reduced economic efficiency at the cost of economic growth, diverted resources into wasteful nonproductive channels, and rewarded incompetence, corruption, and political favoritism.

Supporters of development from below tended to distrust and disparage the motives and the capabilities of governments and of profit-seeking private enterprise, both of which exploit the people in similar ways. They glorified the unrealized potentials of grassroots communities and voluntary associations to empower their members and solve their own problems by self-reliant collective initiative. The process would be participatory and democratic, and the outcome would be the satisfaction of social and material needs as defined by the intended beneficiaries of development strategies. Thus the competing strategies for development came to be clothed with heavy layers of ideological armor, each proclaiming its particular perspective as the unique and exclusive path to economic salvation.

In their more pragmatic, less evangelistic moods, partisans of these three strategies have been prepared to concede that these caricatures have practical limitations. Except for the Stalinist fringe, advocates of state-centered strategies have been willing to concede that for many economic tasks, private enterprise in farming, manufacturing, and commerce is likely to perform more productively and efficiently than state enterprises and that governments should facilitate their activities through market-based incentives. They have also acknowledged the potential of local initiative through voluntary associations, as long as such associations do not challenge the hegemonic role of the state or the stability of existing regimes. Spokespeople for private enterprise were prepared to concede a necessary if limited role for the state in establishing policy frameworks favorable to private initiative, protecting property, enforcing contracts, preventing monopoly, and providing essential public services, including education, transportation, and sanitation. They argued that taxes, however, should be kept low and subsidies that distort market processes should be avoided or minimized. They had no objection to cooperatives and other forms of voluntary initiative, especially if these substituted for government and were free of state subsidies. Partisans of development from below conceded some need for government, especially for activities on a scale and at levels of technological complexity that precluded action by local organizations, as long as they, and private enterprise as well, recognized the primacy of self-managed local institutions as service providers at the local level wherever this was feasible. Governments could "wholesale" resources and services that would then be managed at the retail level by local associations.

These contending ideologies engaged the honest convictions of participants and attentive publics in industrialized as well as Third World countries. Implicit in these ideologies are very practical questions, including relative power and control over resources among politicians and government officials, businesspeople and capitalists, and leaders of community and voluntary associations. The more strident the ideological claims, the more these competing interests tended to be expressed in uncompromising zero-sum language. In many countries, these disputes had ethnic implications as well, since private wealth and business skills on the one hand and government office holding on the other were seldom equally distributed among ethnic communities (Schermerhorn 1970; Horowitz 1985). The vigorous promotion of the free-market model by Western governments and by the World Bank, often as a condition for extending desperately needed financial assistance, seemed to government elites to be designed to shift power in their societies to businesspeople, foreign as well as indigenous, and to align local business interests with foreign interference in national sovereignty, a form of neoimperialism. Thus disputes over appropriate models of development involved not merely ideological preferences or technical issues of economic efficiency, but ultimate control over economic and political resources. The political dimensions of economic strategies have been especially transparent to the main actors in LDCs.

During the 1970s, spokespeople for these governments propagated an elaborate rationale that imputed their economic shortfalls primarily to external neocolonial dependency, to exploitative international economic regimes that extracted low prices for Third World commodities, blocked the entry of finished products to the markets of industrialized countries, monopolized modern production technologies, and denied them access to investment funds and foreign assistance in sufficient quantity and on reasonable terms (Amin 1976; Frank 1972). These grievances were reduced to an ideology that was endorsed by the United Nations General Assembly as a program for a "New International Economic Order" (Sauvant and Hasenpflug 1977).

Spokespeople for the industrialized countries, in contrast, tended to ascribe the economic failures of Third World countries primarily to internal factors—perverse economic policies that penalized production, subsidized consumption, discouraged private enterprise, and proliferated inefficient, overstaffed, and undermotivated departments and enterprises in the public sector (World Bank 1987). Why could not most Third World countries capitalize on opportunities in the expanding international economy, like their successful counterparts in Korea, Taiwan, Malaysia, and Thailand, instead of blaming their problems on outsiders, foreign exploitation, and international institutions?

This ideological standoff dissolved during the 1980s with the recognition that low and unstable commodity prices were hurting and continue to penalize many developing countries, but that their basic problems, like those in the Soviet Union, should be blamed less on outside factors than on unworkable economic policies and practices plus serious deficiencies in management, especially in the institutions and organizations of the state. There is now a broad consensus that priority must be assigned to addressing the critical internal problems of economic policy and management.

EMERGENCE OF A PRAGMATIC CONSENSUS

The economic agony of the 1980s, the widespread increase in deprivation and suffering, and the palpable declines in living standards in many LDCs have prompted a desperate search for economic policies and arrangements that can work, that can overcome economic stagnation, generate employment, increase output, and restore fiscal solvency to the state. The result has been the relaxation of ideological rigor; an inclination to compromise; a greater willingness, especially among government elites, to consider and to try new approaches and fresh policies; and an openness to pragmatic measures that allow greater scope for private enterprise and market forces. The examples of Chinese, Soviet, and Eastern European leadership in experimenting with private initiative and market incentives have been impressive, while the passing of the Reagan-Thatcher era has opened space for less dogmatic approaches from Western sources. As a result of harsh economic necessity and a renewed openness to pragmatic measures, we may be witnessing the end or at least the suspension of ideology concerning strategies for Third World development and the emergence of a new era of consensus politics.

The first sign of this new pragmatism is the increased willingness among participants and analysts alike to address economic performance of the state as an empirical question that may vary from country to country and even with successive regimes in the same country. Where empirical evidence highlights incompetence or resistance to economic rationality, the presumption is to seek and develop competence outside government, in market processes or in local and voluntary associations. Where governments manifest integrity and ability, they can safely be entrusted with a wide range of responsibilities. Choices regarding governmental regulation or participation in economic activities and relations between the state and markets are to be made at the margin in response to pragmatic judgments, rather than as deductions from absolutist ideological positions.

The extravagant claims of the ideologues on all sides have broken down in their confrontation with the complex reality of development. This reality has highlighted not only the limitations and dysfunctions of governments, but also the simultaneous fragility of markets and of private economic initiatives and the weaknesses of local associational capacities when confronted with the challenges of economic stagnation. The experience of the 1980s has underscored the tendency of governments to overreach their financial and managerial capacities, while overlooking and often thwarting capabilities present or latent in society. Yet the fact remains that initiatives from nongovernmental sources are often feeble and unreliable; even when they show signs of vigor, they depend heavily on policies, supports, and services that only agencies of the state can supply. Sustained action oriented to economic development requires continual exchanges between the institutions of state and society. The enactment of policies and the delivery of services by government cannot be effective unless they evoke responsive behavior by the segments of society to which they are addressed. Likewise, initiatives from private enterprise or local associations are likely to falter in the absence of complementary services and supports by government. As these vital interactions and interdependencies come to be appreciated, the dogmatic and exclusive claims of the ideologues on all sides lose their credibility.

Thus the beginning of wisdom in the shaping of development strategies is to abandon as guides to action the dogmatic ideologies that have confounded development policy and management in recent years. The fundamental reality that should shape the management of social and economic development is the essential interdependence of governments, markets, and voluntary action. Their relationships do not constitute zero-sum competition, but rather complementarities that have to evolve in specific patterns for each sector of social and economic activity. Market institutions, government institutions, and community institutions all need to be activated and strengthened, while supportive linkages among them need to be shaped and cultivated. Capabilities to mobilize and use resources, to invest, to operate facilities, and to provide services need to be identified and fostered in each of the sectors that contribute to societal development.

A certain amount of competition and of redundancy among government agencies, private entrepreneurs, and voluntary associations is inevitable, even desirable. Through experience, however, viable divisions of labor and complementarities are likely to emerge. Since managerial capacities represent what is often the scarce and critical factor, the ability to design and sustain purposeful collective action, managerial skills and management institutions need to be identified, enhanced, and released in every sector of society. Presumptions about sources of initiative and the kinds of linkages that should be formed ought, where possible, to be based on pragmatic tests of where the greater competence seems to lie, and they may well differ from place to place and issue to issue. This has been the underlying premise of mixed economies in industrialized societies, and it is especially relevant to LDCs, where capabilities and incentives to mobilize resources and to manage complex activities are in very short supply. The logic of the service networks that emerge from this pluralistic pattern of development management is one of the main themes that will be elaborated in this book. Development management is at the nexus of the ongoing dialectic between state and society.

THE STATE AND THE BURDEN OF ADJUSTMENT

A priori claims for precedence—not to mention monopoly—as the prime mover of development for the state through its bureaucracies, or the market through private enterprise, or popular initiatives through local associations are therefore not helpful in this emerging, more pragmatic environment. In view of enormous needs and limited capacities, there is ample space for development initiatives from all these sources. The burden of adjustment, however, does not fall equally on all parties. Given the demonstrated tendency of most Third World elites to promote state initiatives and of governments to overextend their reach well beyond their financial and managerial capabilities at heavy cost to economic efficiency and to displace other sources of initiative, the burden of self-limitation must, for the balance of this century at least, fall primarily on governments. For even after states yield the operation of manufacturing and commercial enterprises to private firms and of collective farms to peasant proprietors, allow most prices to be set by market processes, and facilitate the provision of certain services by local associations, their remaining responsibilities will more than challenge their financial and managerial capabilities. Substantial shrinkage in the overblown ambitions and operations of the state can actually increase its effectiveness as an agent of social and economic development.

States will necessarily remain central actors in development policy and development management. They must mobilize revenues through taxation, customs, and borrowing; manage public finances, including foreign exchange; and allocate and control substantial funds for a myriad of government-sponsored programs. They must construct, operate, and maintain the essential physical infrastructure of ports, roads, bridges, electric power, water supply, and telecommunications. They must provide for public education and environmental sanitation. They must sponsor agricultural research and extension, conserve land and forest resources, protect the natural environment, and maintain institutions that ensure social order, protect lives and property, enforce contracts, and guarantee the security needed to foster investment and facilitate economic transactions. These are development-related activities that even minimalist governments must undertake, excluding industrial promotion and the numerous welfare-related activities that modern governments are pressured to undertake, if only on a modest scale. Any redistribution of resources or of opportunities in the interest of equity toward deprived classes, disadvantaged regions, or discontented ethnic communities must be initiated and implemented by the state, since markets by their inherent logic are ill-equipped to handle redistributive activities. This applies, for example, to programs intended to improve the social status and recognize and reward the economic roles of women (Dwyer and Bruce 1988; Charlton, Everett, and Staudt 1989).

To finance these responsibilities, states in LDCs must extract fifteen to twenty percent of gross national product (GNP) in revenues. As the largest employer by far, especially of educated manpower, they must recruit, deploy, motivate, compensate, and control a civil service dispersed territorially and through specialized bureaucratic structures that are essential to the performance of public services but are vulnerable to overstaffing, incompetence, abuse of power, corruption, nepotism, and similar failings.

The managerial tasks confronting these governments are enormous, even when full allowance is made for maximum participation by private enterprise and voluntary associations (Bryant and White 1982). The management of the resources and the implementation of activities that are inextricably associated with the state are challenges of very great consequence that can make vital differences in the lives of tens of millions of people. Neither capital alone, nor modern skills and institutions alone, nor sound economic policies alone are sufficient to promote and sustain the development process. All are needed, but in the absence of competent management *in the public sector*, these other capabilities cannot yield the desired developmental outcomes. What, then, are the content and the scope of the concept of public-sector management for development that will inform this book?

ADMINISTRATION, MANAGEMENT, AND LEVELS OF ANALYSIS

Among students and writers concerned with the public sector, the terms "administration" and "management" have been employed interchangeably, the distinctions between them being imprecise and even idiosyncratic. To the founders of the development administration movement in the late 1950s, public administration for development or development administration included the higher-level tasks of senior public officials—shaping policy, taking decisions, and supervising the implementation of government activities oriented not to normal routines, but to the promotion of social and economic development (Riggs 1971). Management, by inference, was a more limited concept involving the details of government procedures and the routines of program implementation. Most of the literature and the courses of instruction on development administration established internationally, many of them in LDCs' universities and institutes of public administration, seemed to accept this conventional distinction between administration and management.

Beginning in the 1980s, and for arcane reasons that have eluded this author, the connotation of these two terms seems to have switched. "Management" is now on top, while "administration" implies subordinate, instrumental routines. I have been advised by younger colleagues that I have all along been thinking and writing about public-sector *management* for development, not *administration*. In deference to the prevailing preference, this is the term that I use in this book to describe and analyze the phenomena that at one time I was pleased to designate as development administration. To most laypeople and practitioners, these terms remain effectively interchangeable. Schools of business administration and of business management teach the same subjects; somewhat different subjects are taught at institutions that designate themselves as schools of public management or schools of public administration. This terminological confusion was nicely finessed by the U.S. government two generations ago when a Division of Administrative Management was established in the Bureau of the Budget under the Executive Office of the President.

When we address the reality of public-sector management oriented to development, we encounter a real problem: the appropriate level or levels of analysis. In some circles, especially among economists, public-sector management refers to the macro management of the national economy. It focuses on the economic policy framework and on specific policy instruments by which economic incentives are believed to be enhanced and economic behavior is regulated and disciplined. The management of the economy is a matter of the right policy choices that determine how the many and diverse economic actors, in the private sector as well as in government, will behave. The concept of public management among some development economists once involved government-sponsored and -sanctioned economic planning and the channeling of resources, especially for investment, according to priorities set by the plan (Waterston 1965). With the current ascendancy of neoclassical economics, the main managerial tasks are to get prices right and allow competitive markets to do their job. In either case, the expectation is that macroeconomic policies can leverage widespread responses among numerous individual economic actors—producers, traders, and consumers. Macroeconomic management, however, functions at a level of activity somewhat remote from the main operations of government.

The next level of analysis and action involves concrete policies and programs by which the state provides public services and promotes and regulates certain forms of economic and social behavior, while maintaining the institutions and instrumentalities of government. This is the range of activities that engages the efforts of most government employees and to which all modern states commit their funds. They extend from public works to agriculture, education, health and sanitation, and urban affairs. Within each of these sectors may be several programs or discrete projects; related sets of activities are administered by specialized bureaucracies and aggregated into departments for purposes of planning, operations, and control. Most of these activities are dispersed over territorial space, requiring the presence of government staff in field stations supervised by bureaucratic hierarchies (Smith 1985). Most of the effort of government officials, whether they are employed by line departments or by semiautonomous public corporations (parastatals), involves the management of resources provided by government. These same activities, however, require continuous interaction with private enterprises, local communities and associations, and individual members of the public. The concept of public management has usually focused on the rules and practices by which government-sponsored programs are designed, implemented, and evaluated.

The third level of analysis and of action, the micro level of management, refers to the operations of individual enterprises, farms, households, communities, and local associations. With the significant exception of local governments, whose developmental role in most LDCs has been quite limited, most of these entities are in private hands, independent centers of decision and action. This is the level of management that most directly affects the great majority of people in their daily lives. These entities may be directly affected for better or worse by macroeconomic policies and by the operations of government agencies. This is not, however, the level of activity normally included in the concept of public administration or public-sector management.

The focus of concern in this book is the large intermediate band between macroeconomic management and the great variety of individual micro-level entities. It includes the functionally specialized sectors and programs of action that are authorized by, controlled by, and accountable to the state; staffed by officials and employees of government; and financed by funds provided directly by government or subject to government control and supervision. In addition to "line" activities that extract resources, regulate behavior, and produce and deliver services, this includes such "staff" or auxiliary services as the allocation and control of public expenditures, the management of public employment, and the procurement of goods and services for use by government agencies. Management at this level also covers the governance of territorially delimited authorities below the level of the state; this usually involves efforts to develop a particular region or to integrate specialized services within its boundaries.

This vast array of state-sponsored activities—functionally specialized line programs, staff services, and territorially based operations—constitutes the domain of public-sector management as conceived in this book. Macroeconomic policies provide part of the policy context within which these affairs are conducted. Development managers may exert considerable influence over the shaping and elaboration of such policies and are mainly responsible for their implementation. On the other hand, the innumerable micro-level units that own, control, and manage most of the resources available to society are the objects of taxation and regulation and the intended beneficiaries of the services sponsored by the state. In some cases, they serve as intermediaries between government and individual members of society. Many micro-level entities are linked with government agencies through complex patterns of interaction and transactions in the networks that exchange information and resources and extend services well beyond the range that governments can normally reach.

Development managers must occupy themselves not only with the internal affairs of the organizations for which they are directly responsible, but also with the external environment that is relevant to their mission. Public-sector managers at the sector and program levels may try to influence macro-level policy decisions and especially budgetary allocations, but for the most part, these must be accommodated and accepted as givens that constrain the management of activities for which these managers are responsible. They must maintain their organization, ensuring its viability and capacity to perform. They must supervise the performance of their substantive regulatory or service activities. And they must respond to and attempt to influence the behavior of other organizations with which they interact in the implementation of their programs—the challenge of linkage management (elaborated in Chapters 5 and 6). These several functions of development may require divisions of labor in senior ranks in all but the smallest organizations. Public-sector managers are normally not involved in the management of micro-level units in society, although they must be aware of circumstances within those important segments of their external environment. This includes the needs, preferences, and convenience of their "clients" or publics. They attempt to affect behavior in micro-level entities, as such entities exert what influence they can to shape government services and regulations to their interests, preferences, and convenience.

Take, for example, the vital field of agriculture. Third World governments sponsor and provide an array of services intended to implement policies that facilitate the production and marketing of crops, livestock, and forest products. Some of these activities are organized as functionally specialized programs within a line department of agriculture; examples of such programs are research and extension, plant protection, and range management. Other activities may be organized as public-sector enterprises, for example, a farm credit or crop marketing corporation; others may be structured on a territorial basis, to develop the agricultural potential of a particular watershed or region. All of them are subject to an economic policy regime, including interest rates and foreign exchange availability, that may constrain budgetary allocations, determine the prices of inputs, and affect the marketability of crops, thereby conditioning the incentives governing producers, processors, and marketers at the micro level.

These agricultural sector illustrations could be extended to the construction and maintenance of highways, health and sanitation, the promotion of small industry, and similar activities sponsored and managed by the state. Government itself and public-sector management are inherently pluralistic phenomena, a concept that will be elaborated in the next chapter. The managers of all such programs do, however, face the common problems of designing, implementing, and controlling activities that are authorized and financed by the state, constrained by public law, accountable to government, and impact on particular microentities or segments of the public. Within the public sector, these diverse activities may be more or less integrated by common governmentwide rules and practices or by routine or ad hoc coordinating arrangements. The middle band of activities— between macrosocietal and macroeconomic policies on the one hand and the numerous households and enterprises that make up the primary units of society—constitutes the pluralistic realm of public-sector management that is the subject of this book.

The reader will have noted that the scope of development management as sketched in this chapter is limited to the executive arms of the state, those entities that are responsible for implementing the policies and programs of government. Legislative and judicial organs of the state are excluded, not because their functions are uninteresting or unimportant, but because most of their activities are not managerial. The same applies to political parties and interest groups, essential as they are to democratic political development and to what many observers believe to be a fundamental ongoing transition from authoritarian to democratic polities in Eastern Europe and many LDCs, especially in Latin America. Although parliaments, courts, and political organizations need to be managed, this is a modest dimension of their roles (Baaklini and Heaphey 1977; Loewenberg and Patterson 1979). As this book is not a text in comparative politics, and as its scope already cries out for tighter boundaries, it seems reasonable to limit the concept of public-sector management to the executive regulatory and service-providing agencies of the state.

DEVELOPMENT MANAGEMENT
VS.
MANAGEMENT DEVELOPMENT

As interest in this subject has expanded, two competing perspectives have emerged. The first focuses on the development of managerial capabilities and institutions. Underlying this approach is the assumption that once capabilities are in place, the various entities in the public sector will be endowed with the ability to undertake the developmental tasks that government requires, to use resources efficiently, to solve fresh problems as they arise, and to sustain increasingly complex and sophisticated activities over time. This, in brief, constitutes the capacity-strengthening and institution-building perspective in development management (Honadle and Van Sant 1986). The other approach emphasizes the management of concrete development activities, arguing that the public sector must concentrate on performance—on delivering the goods, meeting needs, and providing tangible benefits. These shorter-term exigencies, it is argued, must take priority in the allocation of resources and energies over long-term capacity building; indeed, successful experience in program operations and in concrete problem solving is the surest way to develop and sustain managerial capacity.

Taking sides on this issue is not likely to be productive. Long-term capacities must be developed in government and in the private realm. As these capacities are unlikely to evolve spontaneously, governments must be prepared to invest in individual and organizational capabilities. At the same time, policies must be carried out, programs must be operated, and services must be delivered with such managerial resources as exist. Both objectives must be pursued simultaneously, not as trade-offs but as complementary measures. Therefore I look upon development management as comprising both the strengthening of managerial capabilities that can sustain complex activities through time and changing circumstances and the ongoing management of development programs in the public sector.

In LDCs, however, there is a special need to prevent the longer-term development of human skills and institutional capacities from being overwhelmed in the behavior of governments and of external donors as well by short-term programmatic exigencies. What most distinguishes advanced societies and their governments is not their "culture," nor their natural endowments, nor the availability of capital, nor the rationality of public policies, but precisely the capacities of their institutions and the skills of individuals, including those of management. Together these reflect their differential capacities to utilize resources, capitalize on opportunities, and adjust to changes. The availability of these capacities to act in the otherwise impoverished economies of Eastern Europe is what tempts the World Bank and other donors to shift resources from Asia, Africa, and Latin America to Eastern Europe, the expectation being that aid funds will be used more productively where action capacities, including human skills and institutions, are better developed. Thus, while ongoing operations must, of course, be implemented with what capabilities exist, it is critical to the future of LDCs that substantial energies and resources be dedicated to and invested in the enhancement of the human resources and institutional capacities that determine the ability of societies to achieve and sustain economic development. In an important sense, this is what development is all about. For that reason, the emphasis in this book tilts decidedly in the direction of capacity enhancement, especially in the field of public management.

HIERARCHY AND ITS ALTERNATIVES

Both the literature and the practice of classical public administration reflect a pronounced hierarchical, top-down bias. This is a consequence of the persistent nineteenth-century doctrine of state sovereignty—which all contemporary Third World elites have adopted—and the derivation of administrative law from this concept. Public administration is, in one dimension, an expression of the sovereignty of the state. Policies are determined and enunciated at the political levels of government; programs are shaped and refined by senior administrators. They are implemented through centralized bureaucratic hierarchies that enforce accountability upward from subordinate to senior officials. Citizen influence is exercised, when this is feasible, through the political process by elections, political party channels, and interest groups. In relation to state bureaucracies, the public is on the receiving end of regulations and services designed by remote but politically responsible officials. Because of this remoteness, readily construed as neglect and even exploitation, the state and its agents are often experienced and perceived by publics in LDCs as irrelevant and even harmful to their interests and needs.

This hierarchical pattern necessarily reflects the perspectives, preferences, and convenience of senior administrators acting in the name of their political superiors. The perspective from below, however, may be entirely different, since the specific needs, preferences, and convenience of "client" publics cannot as a practical matter be consulted through centralized patterns of decision making and operation; neither can the knowledge or experience of managers or civil servants below the senior ranks, and certainly not those on the ground who are in contact with the public, though they are responsible for the actual implementation of government-sponsored programs. The best they can do is to interpret rules and procedures in practical ways that seem adaptable to specific local situations, to get the job done in a manner not inconsistent with standard top-down instructions. The same discretion that permits needed flexibility may, however, also occasion corruption, favoritism, and similar abuses.

By the standard criteria of effectiveness and efficiency, not to mention responsiveness to public preferences, a strong case can be made for incorporating perspectives from the public and from middle-level and ground-level civil servants. How can such bottom-up perspectives be introduced into development management while the necessities of accountability, control, and even equity are likely to continue to require a considerable measure of centralized decision making and hierarchical administration? The need to relax the prevailing top-down bias in order to accommodate more input from below, from the public and from working levels of state bureaucracies, must be addressed in any meaningful treatment of development management. This too is a theme that will be explored and elaborated in this book.

THE CHALLENGE OF DEVELOPMENT MANAGEMENT

After a slow start, marked by limited effort and considerable skepticism, the development community—leaders of Third World governments as well as donor agencies—has come to accept development management as a necessary component of economic and social development. The importance of management and the priority attached to it have been more evident to the political and administrative elites of Third World countries than to most of the development assistance agencies. The latter have been dominated by economists to whom correct economic policies and investment allocations have been the keys to efficient resource utilization and economic growth. Their tendency to overlook and even disparage administration has been reinforced by sectoral specialists for whom the right technical choices in agriculture, engineering, and medicine are of decisive importance.

Recently, however, major donor agencies have begun to recognize that the paralysis of many of the policy reforms they have promoted and the recurring failures of many of the projects they sponsor and finance, including the inability of governments to sustain them after donors have terminated their assistance, have been due to inept implementation by governments, including serious deficiencies in management. Often the management dimension had not been attended to in the shaping of policies or in project design, or had been attached only as an afterthought. Rhetorical recognition of the management factor has seldom been matched either by increased priority in design or by addition to their staffs of specialists in development management. Modest progress has, however, been realized, including the establishment in the World Bank of small public-sector management units in three of its regional bureaus and of a central policy unit operating under the rubric of "institutional development." More recently, the United Nations Development Program (UNDP) has launched a $60 million Management Development Program. Vague references to deficiencies in "governance" is further recognition that donor-assisted development will continue to be thwarted unless the problems of management capabilities and managerial performance are directly addressed.

The modest but persistent attention to these problems over three decades by a small and scattered cadre of scholars and scholar-practitioners has produced a body of theoretically and empirically based knowledge that is available to inform both policy and practice. Until the late 1970s, the bulk of this research and writing was produced by Western, principally American, scholars. Many of them had been involved in technical-assistance activities in Third World countries. Originally, most of the concepts they employed and the practices they promoted drew heavily on Western rationalist paradigms of bureaucratic administration that were believed to be universally valid (Montgomery 1962; Rondinelli 1987). Their intellectual repertory was, however, soon enriched by behavioral perspectives inspired by the social sciences, by cross-cultural insights, and by anthropological notions that emphasized local distinctiveness, the latent managerial capacities in local societies, and the importance of local commitment to management reforms and development (Esman and Montgomery 1969). The intellectual capital now available to students and practitioners of development management is rich and varied.

Development administration gradually achieved the status of a minor branch of the field of public administration. Respectable academic journals were dedicated to this subject; a section on international and comparative administration functions as an active autonomous unit of the American Society for Public Administration. In addition, much useful writing, especially in public health and rural development, was produced by specialists in substantive fields, with little or no formal training in administration or management (Mosher 1975; Bossert and Parker 1982). Recently a growing volume of published work, based on local research and experience, has been produced by Third World scholars, many of them trained at the graduate level in U.S. universities and affiliated with departments and institutes of public administration in their own countries (Kiggundu 1989; Garcia-Zamor 1977; Inayatullah 1976). Although most of their concepts have been drawn from the Western tradition, concepts and practices derived from indigenous experience will increasingly be represented in their writing, contributing to practical guidance and enriching the science of comparative administration.

During the past decade, students of development management have begun to emphasize the learning dimension of applied work in this discipline (Korten 1980). Program managers in LDCs are likely to encounter a high degree of uncertainty about the results that specific interventions can yield, uncertainty about natural conditions, public response to program interventions, and the behavior of implementing organizations. Because of the prevailing uncertainty and the risk of unanticipated consequences, program interventions in Third World situations should never be treated as architectural blueprints. They should instead be regarded as action hypotheses subject to modification and adjustment resulting from systematic monitoring, periodic evaluation of processes as well as outputs, and learning from specific experience (Rondinelli 1983). Formal knowledge from the professional literature is one source of guidance; learning from concrete situations is another; the experience and judgment of front-line civil servants and of members of the "client" publics is a third source of information about what is likely to work in specific situations. Development managers must be prepared to draw on and integrate these three categories of knowledge. Uncertainty about the natural and social environment can be reduced by the careful collection and analysis of local information both before and during program implementation, a process that can be facilitated by the participation of affected publics (Whyte and Boynton 1983; Cohen and Uphoff 1977). This can be an aid and a supplement, but never a substitute for experiential learning and willingness to adjust program operations accordingly.

My intention in this book is to draw liberally on all these sources but to shape this body of knowledge in directions that I believe will be especially relevant as the twenty-first century approaches. Although this presentation will be experience based, I intend to maintain it at a sufficient level of generality and abstraction that it can be broadly applicable to the circumstances of most LDCs. There is, of course, great diversity among these countries, a few of which have "graduated" during the past decade or so beyond that circle and have joined the ranks of newly industrializing countries (NICs). I do not intend to become embroiled in definitions about the precise properties and exact boundaries of Third World states and societies. Nor is this general work a substitute for intensive country analyses or for more bounded case studies. My objective, instead, is to make general statements that account for and explain a wide range of experiences and to prescribe courses of action that can be applied productively to concrete problems of development management.

One caution, however, is indicated at this point. The management dimension of development necessarily imposes heavy burdens of leadership and enterprise on senior managers as individuals and as a group. There is, consequently, a temptation to which some writers succumb: to hope for charismatic qualities among development managers because their responsibilities are so heavy and the processes of social change in which they are major participants are so demanding. When charisma or genius appears in managerial ranks, this is indeed a fortunate accident, for men and women so endowed may by the strength of their personalities inspire extraordinary performance from others. But no realistic prescription for large-scale collective action can anticipate or rely on the availability of genius; this defies statistical probability. Managerial leadership must instead emerge from persons of above-average talent, which, unlike genius, is available at all times in all societies. Their skills can be shaped by education and experience, their devotion to duty can be evoked by a professional ethos into which they have been socialized and that is continuously reinforced, and their performance can be stimulated by an appropriate regime of incentives and rewards. A prescription for leadership roles should impose exacting requirements on cadres of above-average men and women, but if leadership roles depend on charisma, performance will always fall short, because the supply of persons so endowed is severely limited in all societies and cannot be predicted.

I was once responsible for identifying and launching the training of development managers in Malaysia, a country that has been conspicuously successful in economic development (Esman 1972a). A generation later, these managers occupy a large number of the senior management posts in the Malaysian government. These people were well above average in natural talent; they were well-educated, highly motivated, and generously compensated, but none could have been characterized as charismatic. They have, however, provided outstanding managerial leadership to the organizations responsible for Malaysia's state-led development programs. Development management roles should be designed to challenge and reward persons of this caliber who are likely to be available for competitive recruitment and career development. But to design, for public-sector management, leadership roles so demanding that only persons of genius can satisfactorily fill them is a sure prescription for frustration and futility.

Development management is a social enterprise that benefits from excellent leadership in the public sector, but this must be matched by efforts that evoke similar leadership in nongovernmental organizations dispersed throughout society. Professional management cadres in government can, however, stimulate and assist in the development and diffusion of attitudes, skills, and institutions that are conducive to effective managerial behavior in other sectors of society, a topic that will be examined in Chapters 5 and 6.

2

SOCIETAL DIFFERENTIATION, BUREAUCRATIC PLURALISM, AND THE THIRD WORLD STATE

THE CENTRALIZING IMPERATIVE

THE COMMANDING PRIORITY FOR THE POLITICAL ELITES OF LESS DEVELOPED countries (LDCs) is to consolidate and maintain the hegemony of their regimes. There are other goals as well, such as economic development, the cultivation of interethnic harmony, and the spread of education and enlightenment, but these must always be consistent with and subordinate to the imperative need for the survival and consolidation of their rule. With this in mind, the strong and invariant tendency of such regimes has been to centralize power in the hands of the state and its agencies, intending thereby to reinforce their control. In economic decision making they may displace market processes with networks of administrative controls, subsidies, and regulations; often they preempt financial, manufacturing, and commercial operations from enterprises and firms and transfer these functions to agencies of government. They may strip local government authorities of their taxing powers and of their responsibilities for local services and transfer them to the administrative organs of the state. Centralized control, they believe, is a necessary strategy for ensuring the strength and stability of the state, for neutralizing or eliminating potential competitors for power, for promoting modernization and national unity, and for countering the centrifugal effects of ethnic pluralism.

Yet these states seldom display sufficient capacities to match the ambitions of their rulers (Wunsch and Olowu 1990). Economic policies that have the effect of concentrating control in the state are frequently ill-conceived and self-defeating, stifling the incentives of investors and producers. The operations of large economic enterprises owned by the state often compound managerial failures with economic policies that thwart incentives for efficiency, turn out mediocre products, and impose financial burdens on the state treasury, thereby guaranteeing chronic dependency and eventual bankruptcy (Nellis 1986; Ramanadham 1984). Due to financial and managerial limitations, the ability of agencies of the state to penetrate society with enforceable regulations or useful services often falls far short of their intentions with perverse effects, because they displace previous providers of similar services. Competition for subsidies and efforts to evade controls divert energies from production and marketing to political manipulation and provide incentives for bribery and similar corrupt practices.

During two decades of economic growth from about the mid-1950s until the mid-1970s, the managerial capacities of most Third World states did increase incrementally as their administrative institutions took root and gained valuable experience, while the qualifications of staff members improved. State budgets, supplemented by grants and loans from foreign and international assistance agencies and from commercial banks, provided funds to order equipment, procure supplies, and add personnel, thus extending the range of government regulatory, service, and enterprise operations. Management struggled with indifferent success to keep pace with the expanding activities of the centralizing state. And then the bubble burst.

Acute strains on state finances resulting from the cumulative effects of the oil shock, the collapse of commodity prices, and the debt crises of the early 1980s brought an abrupt end to the expansion of the state's reach. In economically more favored and better managed states—Thailand, Malaysia, Chile, and Togo, for example—government activities contracted slightly; in the most severely affected countries, the state's capacities were so eroded that its presence in many areas of society nearly vanished. Hospitals were no longer supplied with essential drugs, road maintenance virtually ceased, there was no fertilizer to distribute, and civil servants could no longer support their families on salaries that had been stripped of their real value by uncontrolled inflation.

Thus governments confront a harsh dilemma. Their continuing impulse is to accumulate decision-making powers and operational responsibilities in the hands of the state and to expand and centralize them, thereby consolidating and stabilizing regimes that remain uncertain of the scope and depth of their legitimacy in the societies over which they attempt to exercise control. The past few years have demonstrated, however, the limitations of their financial and managerial capacities to exercise the powers they claim. It now appears that governments were unwise ever to have ventured into some of these areas; in others, their capacities are unlikely to expand fast enough to close the existing gap. The resolution of this dilemma is critical to the survival of regimes and to their ability to promote and support social and economic development. It is pregnant with consequences for development management. I shall explore methods for reconciling the insecure elites of these countries with the implications of their limited financial and management capacities without jeopardizing the viability of their regimes or compromising their developmental roles. This will require reconcentration on the core activities of government and relaxation of the centralizing tendencies of the post–World War II and early independence era.

SOCIETAL DIFFERENTIATION

The limited capacities of Third World states are further complicated by the highly differentiated and poorly integrated composition of the societies they are attempting to govern. The various publics that these states must attempt to serve and control often have little in common. The phenomenon of economic dualism is well recognized: "modern" enclaves that include mostly urban-based government offices, banks, factories, and trading houses, along with a few large-scale farming operations; "traditional" low-productivity occupations that involve the great majority of households—small-scale artisans, traders, and service providers in the urban "informal" sector, and numerous subsistence smallholders, tenants, and laborers in rural areas. There are few economic linkages between the "modern" and the "traditional" sectors or between various regions of the country. There is a pronounced urban bias in the shaping of policies and provision of government services, social as well as economic (Lipton 1977). Governments tend to appreciate and respond quite unevenly to the needs of their various constituents; most policies and actual allocations favor urban areas whose residents are better able to articulate their preferences, whose life-styles parallel those in the senior ranks of government, and whose grievances can represent a threat to regime stability.

Less understood by outsiders but even more fundamental to the maintenance of the state is the vertical segmentation that characterizes most LDCs. In its more benign form, this pluralism is expressed in patron-client networks that are often based on extended kinship or economic dependency. The state is expected to relate to society and distribute its benefits through these patron-client channels, in exchange for which the patrons deliver their support and the compliance of their clients to the regime. The state selects or works through patrons who can take care of their followers and keep them under control; resources and access provided by government enrich the patron, reinforce the patron's authority, and stabilize the regime.

More problematical are ethnic cleavages that become competitive and politicized (Rothschild 1981; Young 1976). The governance of ethnically plural states may involve the apportionment among ethnic communities of cultural values, including religious and language rights; of economic values, including jobs, contracts, and public investments; and of political values, including participation, representation, and autonomy. When a regime is dominated by a single ethnic community or an ethnic coalition, advantages tend to flow disproportionately to their constituents; ethnic communities that are left out may become aggrieved, alienated, and eventually rebellious. When a regime attempts to incorporate all the component ethnic communities by combinations of consociational devices such as proportionality in the allocation of benefits and regional autonomy, governance involves the continual balancing of competing ethnic demands on the limited resources and capabilities of the state. The primary identification of individuals is with their ethnic community; their adherence to the state is contingent on the satisfaction of their collective symbolic and instrumental expectations and demands. Often ambitious individuals and factions compete for the right to represent their ethnic community in its exchanges with other communities and with the state, each attempting to outdo the other in the range and stridency of their demands.

Further complicating these expressions of societal differentiation are natural factors—differences in the specific microenvironments in which communities function and people attempt to extract their livelihoods. Soils, rainfall, climate, and similar natural factors—including even human, animal, and plant diseases—may differ over small expanses of territory. Even in the absence of societal pluralism, such natural factors may require distinctive treatment and responses by government, confounding the drive toward uniformity that characterizes centralized state administration. If they are to be relevant and responsive to the needs of their publics in their distinctive microenvironments, governments must find ways to adjust the structures and processes of development management accordingly.

This extremely brief and simplified excursion into the sociology of Third World politics has been necessary to demonstrate a simple but fundamental reality. In the context of development management, the state presides over and attempts to intervene in societies that are highly differentiated and poorly integrated. The state is but one source of identity and allegiance, and often a minor influence in the lives of its citizens (Migdal 1988). Among these component social and economic formations, patron-client factions, and ethnic communities, and between any of them and the state, competition is endemic; conflicts may erupt at any time. The avoidance and regulation of these conflicts by combinations of accommodative and coercive means are constant preoccupations of governing elites. The maintenance of their polity takes precedence over concerns with development, and they regard the latter as instrumental to their political needs. More commonly, allocations for development and the management of these activities must take account of the unequal resources and the competing claims of the differentiated publics that are both subjects and constituents of the state.

Development management, like public administration generally, is a dialectical set of interactions between state and society. The rulers who control the machinery of the state attempt to (1) extract resources from society, principally by taxation, in order to finance the operations of government; (2) regulate behavior in ways that maintain the regime while promoting order, health, morality, the integrity of economic transactions, and similar values as defined by government; and (3) provide economic and social services and symbolic satisfactions that respond to public demand, promote the goals of the regime, and thereby ensure acquiescence and, it is hoped, support from those whose needs and expectations are accommodated by public services for which the regime claims credit. Those elements of society that can mobilize and organize themselves for this purpose strive to gain benefits from the state in the form of favorable regulations, responsive policies, and especially particularistic benefits—jobs, university admissions, contracts, subsidies, and government-financed facilities. These government-sponsored "outputs" are achieved by such tactics as promising political and electoral support or threatening the withdrawal of support; exploiting ethnic, kinship, or patron-client ties; and the employment of bribes or similar forms of corrupt inducements. These methods are used at all levels of the state apparatus, from senior politicians and bureaucrats to local agents of the state who control minor allocations and may be vulnerable to pressures from influential local politicians, landlords, or businesspeople. The state must often make expedient concessions to the reality of local power centers.

In these exchanges, however, the state tends to be the more powerful actor. This is because states, even those that are understood to be "soft" states (Myrdal 1968), usually control the ultimate means of coercion, enjoy monopolistic access to foreign aid, serve as gatekeeper for foreign investment and trade, and do not ordinarily depend on public support through periodic competitive elections. Thus they enjoy a measure of autonomy in relation to their society and its diverse publics and can dictate to the latter the effective terms of exchange. To the extent that they are organized, the various publics work within these shifting constraints. Normally they attempt to cajole what benefits they can in the form of advantageous policies or particularistic benefits. If the state and its agents become ineffectual or unduly oppressive, however, sections of the public may attempt to delink or withdraw from the reach of government, seeking thereby to maximize their autonomy and freedom of action from the interference and exactions of authorities that are considered incompetent, exploitative, or needlessly intrusive (Migdal 1988). The visible effects of such withdrawal may be informal barter exchanges, underground transactions including smuggling, reliance on local self-help, and similar efforts to substitute for government activities or to keep its agents at bay.

BUREAUCRATIC INSTITUTIONS

For linking state and society, modern bureaucracies have proved to be the most effective, robust, and reliable instruments and intermediaries. By *bureaucracy*, I refer to hierarchical structures of authority with explicit divisions of labor, formal rules governing flows of work and information, and specific provisions for interaction with the public (Blau 1963). These familiar structures have demonstrated a unique capacity to convert human and material resources to disciplined capabilities and to generate and control action in reasonably predictable patterns over extended time and space. As authoritarian hierarchies operating under explicit rules and through intricate divisions of labor, bureaucratic organizations achieve for the elites of the state a combination of control, accountability, uniformity, and equity that no other system of large-scale organization has been able to match. The formal rules by which bureaucracies operate help political elites to fend off and defend themselves from the particularistic demands of their differentiated publics. For such reasons, all modern governments, without a single exception that I am aware of, employ the bureaucratic form of organization as their mainstay for achieving and sustaining relationships with their various publics.

It is not that politicians, state elites, or members of the public find bureaucratic structures and processes especially appealing, but rather that all the practical alternatives have proved less effective and less reliable. Political party channels, for example, may be useful for communicating information, decisions, and demands, but for the routine enforcement of regulations or delivery of services, they are ineffective and unreliable. When political parties become bureaucratized, as in single-party Leninist-style polities, they are not dependable instruments for the normal operations of government, and their activities tend to be sporadic and arbitrary. Traditional structures such as patron-client and kinship networks are limited in the publics they serve, the technical capacities they can assemble, and the accountability they can maintain. The truth is that, despite their manifold vulnerabilities to failure and abuse, the modern state has found no acceptable substitute for bureaucratic organization and no social invention that can replace it.

Bureaucracy is certainly one of the most unloved social inventions of all time. Everyone deplores it, distrusts it, and yearns for better alternatives. There are shelves of learned publications that delight in cataloging its dysfunctions and in castigating and deploring its inadequacies, pathologies, and abuses. These themes, well summarized by Goodsell (1983), are so familiar to students of public management that I shall not pause to rehearse them here. Economists are deeply hostile to bureaucracy because it appears to encroach on the market mechanisms to which their otherwise dismal science is passionately devoted; political scientists distrust bureaucracy because it appears to limit or displace the electoral, representative, and political processes to which they are committed; sociologists condemn bureaucracy because it regiments and dehumanizes society by formal rules and routines, thereby limiting the spontaneity of social interactions. Politicians are quick to deflect criticisms of their actions or inactions onto faceless bureaucrats who can be safely blamed because their anonymity and hierarchical subordination prevent them from publicly defending themselves.

Bureaucracy is charged, often not inaccurately, with contradictory offenses: with mindless adherence to rigid rules and formal, impersonal routines at the expense of performance and timely responsiveness to public needs, the means—red tape—displacing the goals; with abuse of discretion, resulting in favoritism, discrimination, self-serving enrichment, and corruption; with technical and managerial incompetence that absorbs and squanders scarce resources, while producing few benefits for society and at high cost; with bureaucratic politics, victimizing both state and society in self-regarding struggles for irresponsible power and pelf. State bureaucracies are vulnerable to the political abuses of overstaffing and of employment according to ethnic, nepotistic, or patronage criteria that undermine discipline and performance incentives. So rigid, complex, and often contradictory are the formal rules and procedures in government bureaucracies that only informal behavior outside the rules permits the essential business of government to proceed, but these informal practices invite foot-dragging and corruption.

There is observable truth in all these frequently repeated charges. Yet the effectiveness of development management cannot be advanced by the intellectually and morally futile, sterile, and irresponsible expedient of bureaucrat bashing. Nor can it be advanced, beyond a reasonable point, by attempts to bypass or substitute for state bureaucracies. Some activities can and should be removed from government and committed to market processes and to private enterprise, often, alas, to private-sector bureaucracies. Other activities may be devolved to local authorities or to community or voluntary associations. Privatization and devolution, however, always leave residual roles for government services or regulation that must be managed by bureaucratic agencies. For the bulk of activities that must remain with government, bureaucratic organization, with all its imperfections and vulnerabilities, will continue to be the main instrument of action for states in LDCs, as it has been in all industrialized and Communist systems.

One thesis that I advance in this book is that bureaucratic organization, as a vehicle for development management, has both rough virtues and troublesome defects. As a human institution, it falls far short of the well-oiled production machine conceived by the proponents of scientific management or of the Weberian rational-legal ideal-type structure (Weber 1947). The virtues, however, substantially outweigh the defects, and neither theory nor experience has identified alternative structures that can serve the same set of purposes with anything approaching equal reliability or effectiveness. Therefore, the constructive directions for development management are to (1) identify and implement methods to increase the productivity, effectiveness, and responsiveness of bureaucratic structures and (2) combine the discipline and control that are essential to governmental accountability with operational flexibility needed to accommodate societal differentiation, while (3) controlling and minimizing dysfunctions and abuses and (4) enhancing programmatic linkages among official bureaucratic entities and between state agencies, private economic enterprises, local authorities, and associations in the voluntary and community sectors of society. In the chapters that follow, these themes will be elaborated.

BUREAUCRATIC PLURALISM

The bureaucratic structures of the state constitute the institutional environment in which and through which public development managers function. With their personnel, the authority conferred on them by the state, the material and financial resources entrusted to them, and the information they control, these organizations are the instruments through which development managers, as agents of the state, act on society and respond, in turn, to societal demands. State bureaucracy, however, constitutes a profoundly plural phenomenon. There is no single state bureaucracy, nor can there be. Conventional references to "the" state bureaucracy as an aggregate or collectivity are useless and misleading. Every bureaucratic agency represents a distinctive subculture within the state apparatus. This distinctiveness is a function of the professional training and orientation of the senior staff, of the technologies they employ in producing their outputs, and of the needs, capabilities, and expectations of the particular publics they regulate or serve. Thus the culture of an enterprise that generates and distributes electric power differs markedly from that of a family-planning agency, and both of them differ from a central bank or a department of prisons and corrections.

There are, as I noted in Chapter 1, some integrating forces, among them common requirements for claiming funds and for expenditure control, common procedures for the procurement of supplies and equipment, and common rules and standards governing the employment and compensation of personnel and their working conditions. The effectiveness of these common rules and procedures is, however, quite problematical. The various bureaucracies enjoy a considerable measure of operating autonomy, and this is reinforced by the political weight of their ministers, birds of passage who nevertheless are able to claim discretionary space for the empires of which they are temporarily in charge. The relative autonomy of these vertical, functionally specialized structures, including their inclination to maintain tight boundaries in relation to parallel bureaucracies performing complementary activities, produces one of the classical dilemmas in modern public administration. This is the difficulty of programmatic coordination among bureaucracies charged with complementary, even interdependent, functions that affect the same public—for example, irrigation, farm credit, and agricultural extension, especially at the field level. In Chapter 4, I examine programmatic coordination as a problem in development management.

The daily encounter between bureaucratic pluralism and differentiated publics is one of the main tensions confronting development management. The normal tendency in bureaucracy—as among academic students of public law and administration—is to regard its clientele as an undifferentiated public to whom regulations are to be applied and services delivered uniformly, therefore objectively and equitably. Differentiated publics, on the other hand, expect to be treated according to their distinctive needs and special circumstances. They may, for example, demand that services be provided in their minority language or that certain individuals or groups be accepted as intermediaries between them and government agencies. The intention and the effect are normally to mitigate the impact of regulations, increase their share of benefits, or respond to their particular needs and preferences. They may be abetted in these expectations by the political weight of their spokespeople or by the penetration of members of their own community into the bureaucratic ranks.

Development managers find themselves in the middle, at the point of impact between the propensity for uniformity and control in their bureaucratic headquarters and the particularistic expectations and demands of their differentiated publics. The dimensions of this inherent tension are, of course, variable in their scope and intensity. The resolution of these incongruent expectations involves expedient understandings and techniques of accommodation, usually informal, that test the political skills of development managers. Eligibility for agricultural credit might, for example, be stretched to include a women's cooperative that manufactures and markets handicrafts on grounds that they contribute to the local rural economy while complying with standard rules for the repayment of loans. Although such adjustments may compromise formal patterns of bureaucratic operations, they allow the state-society dialectic to be played out in ways that are more or less tolerable to the concerned parties.

What contributes some coherence and integration to these pluralistic structures and their specialized activities are the processes of management.

Whatever the sector, the core of the management function involves the allocation and control of funds; the deployment, motivation, and supervision of personnel; the production and marketing of public goods and services; the enforcement of accountability and of quality control; the accommodation of publics that consume services; and the cultivation of linkages with external agencies. These are among the common functions and requirements of development managers in whatever sector they operate. It is these common functions and the common skills required in public-sector management, combined with an ethos of public service, that warrant the designation of development management not only as a process but also as a profession. In the hands of incompetent, unmotivated, or corrupt personnel, development management can add up to a net burden on society, consuming in resources more than it provides in benefits; in the hands of committed and highly motivated professionals, even under unpromising political conditions, it can make a decisive contribution to sustained and broadly based social and economic development.

The integrative functions and the professional dimensions of development management are themes that will be explored in subsequent chapters. In no state are they entirely present or entirely absent. The posture of the regime in control of the state provides constraints or opportunities for the exercise of management skills. Development managers can expect to exert some influence, but seldom a determinative influence, on the behavior of political elites, and it is idle to postulate ideal regime behavior as the precondition to optimal management performance. For the most part, managers must function within the constraints, while making the most of the opportunities afforded by the regime under which they operate. Parallel to carrying out their substantive service, regulatory, or enterprise responsibilities, one practical task is the incremental enhancement of the capabilities of individual bureaucracies in which and through which most public-sector managers function; and more broadly, of the interbureaucratic and interinstitutional networks that increasingly constitute the framework for the promotion and implementation of development-related activities.

ON STATE AUTONOMY

A treatise on development management cannot fail to come to grips with the issue that more than any other has preoccupied political scientists during the past decade: the question of the autonomy of the state. Is the state normally free to exercise authority over society, to impose the will and the preferences of its elites and officials (Evans, Rueschemeyer, and Scocpol 1985), or are the actions of government mainly constrained and determined by pressures from organized interests in society (Easton 1965)? To put the matter crudely, can the state, through its bureaucracies, dominate society? Or do societal interests exert effective control over the instrumentalities and actions of the state? This is not a trivial question, for if the state's development managers are mostly captives and tools of societal forces, then they cannot exert independent power; endowed with limited discretion, they become relatively minor, unimportant actors in the development process, implementers of routines, hardly deserving of serious scholarly attention.

In evaluating this controversy, I revert to an earlier observation about state bureaucracy as a plural phenomenon. This being the case, it becomes impossible for "the" bureaucracy to be captured, since each section of the state's executive apparatus confronts different publics endowed with different resources, capabilities, and expectations. The question then comes down to this: For any individual program of action, in what direction does predominant influence run? Is initiative primarily in the hands of one or more state bureaucracies, or in the hands of one or more organized interest groups? With bureaucracy thus disaggregated, as it must be to conform with reality, the question of relative autonomy or capture becomes in every instance an empirical determination. Neither the primitive Marxian notion that the state serves as the agent of the (bourgeois) ruling class, nor the sociological claim that societal forces necessarily determine politics, nor the contrary proposition that the autonomous sovereign state is the dominant actor provides reliable rules for judgment in individual cases.

Empirically, on particular issues and programs, the predominant influence can run in either direction. At one end of the spectrum may be the bureaucratic agency that dominates the administration of a program and reduces its public to total dependency; in such cases there are few countervailing influences from society. At the opposite end is an agency that has been captured by its clientele and is systematically and predictably bent to the latter's interest. Between the theoretical extremes are numerous intermediate combinations of relative influence. An urban housing agency may be in full control of the allocation and management of sites and services in relation to its unorganized public; a department of agriculture and its associated marketing parastatal may be entirely responsive to politically aggressive organizations representing landed interests; an irrigation bureaucracy may be in effective control of the cultivators who depend on it for the reliable supply of a vital production input, but that same department may be extremely sensitive and responsive to large construction contractors who contribute generously to political campaigns and are willing to share some of their profits with senior officials; a ministry of finance may be highly solicitous of the advice and interests of commercial banks, resolving most doubts in their favor, but when circumstances require, that same bureaucracy may impose severe regulatory controls to combat inflation. The direction of influence may shift with changing circumstances.

In general, the better organized the clientele and the more open the polity to societal pressures, the less the autonomy of the state bureaucracies and the greater the influence of organized interest groups. These factors vary from country to country, they vary over time, and they vary with individual sectors and programs of government. Further complicating these relationships may be tensions between politicians and senior bureaucrats, the former more inclined to be responsive to friendly interest groups, the latter more inclined to insist on the integrity of rules and the hegemony of officialdom. It is nonsense to treat these relationships as gross aggregates; the balance between bureaucratic autonomy and societal influences is in every instance an empirical determination.

In treating the dialectic between state and society, there can be no a priori judgments about the direction of influence. In this pluralistic universe, each case must be evaluated by the evidence. In some situations, state bureaucracies may be overresponsive to organized clienteles, even performing at their behest. In others, the state exerts a dominating influence, degenerating at times to exploitation of particular publics by neglect, abuse, or extortion. By sector and program, the state may be overresponsive or underresponsive to relevant publics. In most Third World states, the levels of social mobilization and political activation are relatively modest, the claims of organized interest groups on the state are manageable, and the bureaucracies retain considerable discretion and freedom of maneuverability.[1] The quality of development management can therefore make an important difference in the productivity and quality of life of members of the public; it is not predetermined by politics. Consequently, there is less danger of capture than of insufficient capabilities, managerial and financial; less danger of capture than of governmental overload resulting more from the defective strategies of state elites bent on expanding and consolidating their power than from the demands of organized societal interests.

ON THE WITHERING OF THE MODERN STATE

A number of contemporary scholars and observers, often with the enthusiasm of pristine revelation, argue that the era of the modern territorial state has begun to pass into history, to be supplanted by other patterns of authority. The latter range from the transnational corporation to suprastate structures or to local communitarian associations. Though there is no a priori reason to expect that the modern state will survive indefinitely in its present form, I see little concrete evidence in LDCs that radical transformations are under way. That politically unaccountable, profit-seeking transnational corporations might substitute for the state is a profoundly distressing prospect for any society; but although transnational enterprises will almost certainly be major actors in an interdependent global economy, there is neither evidence that they are displacing the core functions of the state nor any theoretical basis for that expectation; indeed it can be argued that the state is increasingly needed to protect societies from the excesses and abuses of transnational corporations. Devolution of some service and regulatory activities from centralized governments to regional units, local authorities, and voluntary associations is a genuine prospect—indeed it is strongly recommended in this book—but in no instance I am aware of have these entities substituted for the major functions of the state. The Soviet empire and the Indian federation may indeed devolve substantial powers to their constituent regional authorities. Some of them may even achieve political independence, but these successor structures are almost certain to function as territorial states, inheriting and deploying on a smaller scale the powers and functions of their multinational or multiethnic predecessors. The disintegration of the latter does not imply the withering of state power, only its relocation.

The strengthening of the European Economic Community—progressive economic and informational integration with important implications for both social policy and human rights—has not displaced the established states in Western Europe. It has added another arena of politics and administration in which established states remain the principal actors. Outside Europe, efforts to achieve effective supranational cooperative structures with more than consultative functions have been uniformly unsuccessful. The Central American Common Market has collapsed; the very useful East African Common Services Organization has ceased to function. Despite the apparently irrational scale of many contemporary states as economic units and their inability to support separate institutions—for example, for specialized higher education or agricultural research—the creation and maintenance of suprastate structures even for manifestly desirable purposes have been hard to achieve, and successful cases are fragile and rare. While the future may witness the emergence of successful suprastate institutions for specific specialized functions, and while instances of economic and technical cooperation may generate more generalized suprastate structures, there is little reason to expect that these will in significant ways diminish the powers, functions, or roles of the territorial state. That the state is about to wither away is a fanciful proposition, one that, in view of all the visible evidence, should not detain serious students of public affairs (*Economist* 1990). For the most part, these prophecies are grounded in crude and simplistic notions of economic determinism, overlooking the noneconomic functions of the state and even the formidable residual functions of statehood that accompany economic integration.

The implications for development management are clear. The state will continue to be the major political structure within which and through which initiatives oriented to economic and social development are managed. Public development managers will continue to be employed by the state and to work within its imperfect and pluralistic framework. But because of the societal pluralism inherent in all LDCs combined with severe limitations on the operating capacities of the state, political and administrative elites can no longer convincingly claim a monopoly on development initiatives and responsibilities. They must come to terms with and adapt their policies, structures, and procedures to the realities of their task environment as outlined in this chapter. The state will remain an important, but by no means monopolistic, actor; patterns of cooperative and competitive accommodation between state bureaucracies and other segments of society will be worked out and adjusted mainly by public development managers. This will constitute their major challenge, the dimensions of which are a principal theme in the chapters that follow.

NOTES

[1] A conspicuous exception appears to be contemporary India. Scholars writing on that polity argue that the state has been overwhelmed by too much politics, especially by the aggressive demands of caste associations, organized landed interests, and industrial capitalists, that preempt the state's resources and administrative energies (Kohli 1990).

3

BUREAUCRACY AND PROGRAM MANAGEMENT

BUREAUCRATIC ROLES: INSTRUMENTAL, POLITICAL, ENTREPRENEURIAL

BUREAUCRATIC ORGANIZATION IS LIKELY TO REMAIN THE BASIC STRUCTURE within which development managers function and through which management affects society. Ideally, bureaucracy performs like a disciplined machine, converting laws and policies efficiently and predictably to outputs as contemplated by the military model or the rational-legal ideal propounded by Max Weber (1947). Nowhere is this expectation realized, though it is close enough in many Western polities to serve as a rough and credible point of departure for the empirical analysis of administrative institutions and program implementation. In most less developed countries (LDCs), however, distortions of the Weberian norm extend much farther, due to a combination of limited capabilities, perverse incentives, complex and poorly integrated societies, cultural norms that contradict the rational-legal logic of bureaucratic behavior, and political penetration of administrative structures. Under these conditions, the ability of state bureaucracies to carry out the intentions of their political masters or to do so at acceptable levels of efficiency is problematical. Bureaucratic organizations become both indispensable resources and vexing problems (Kiggundu 1989, ch. 1).

Operating through bureaucratic structures, development managers perform several functions. Their manifest function is purely instrumental—to convert public laws and government policies to routine courses of action that enforce regulations and deliver predictable services to specific publics in cost-effective ways. This instrumental role shapes the standard self-image of development managers, as it does of career public administrators everywhere. This is also the role of career executives that is most acceptable to senior politicians and government elites. The late prime minister of

Malaysia, Tun Abdul Razak, once issued these instructions in my presence to a gathering of senior civil servants: "I make the decisions; your job is to implement them faithfully, promptly, and efficiently." The instrumental function has been the main concern of academic observers associated with the discipline of public administration—how to enhance the effectiveness and efficiency of program managers.

More sophisticated observers have long recognized the political function of senior public administrators, including development managers. Through their "advice" to political superiors, their technical and managerial expertise, their control of vital information, their ongoing contacts with relevant publics, they influence the policies and the content of the programs for which they are responsible. They are active players in the competitive struggle for favorable policies and scarce budget resources. In the implementation of programs and in their application to specific circumstances, they decide what information is relevant, and they "interpret" policies and rules in ways that make important differences to members of the public. Indeed, their control of policy and program implementation may, deliberately or inadvertently, produce consequences substantially at variance with those intended by their political masters. These discretionary dimensions of development management are recognized as normal expressions of their unavoidable political function. When, however, their political activities extend to the use of public office for the diversion of government funds to themselves and their associates—political corruption—or to the deployment of bureaucratic influence to affect the disposition of power in the state, then the boundaries of their legitimate political functions may be considered to have been breached. Where this boundary lies in specific situations can be disputed. There can be no disputing the fundamental point that the activities of development managers in influencing policy and controlling implementation include important political dimensions (Lindenberg and Crosby 1981).

In a developmental context, senior managers are expected to perform in a third, entrepreneurial role—that of initiating and facilitating action that would otherwise not occur. Public entrepreneurship includes activating unutilized resources, inspiring and supporting nonroutine behavior, and helping government officials and members of the public to reorient and recombine material and human resources, thereby enabling the achievement of outcomes that had previously been impossible. The conventional image of the rule-bound, risk-averse bureaucratic manager excludes the entrepreneurial function. Yet there is considerable evidence that development managers can and do perform as entrepreneurs; their initiatives and leadership can and do break bottlenecks and make things happen at the level of individual projects, large-scale programs, and the interorganizational and interinstitutional networks that increasingly constitute the arena in which senior development managers operate (Paul 1983). Although government managers are by no means the sole entrepreneurs, their authority, prestige, and control of resources can and should be focused on innovating new and unorthodox ways of addressing concrete developmental tasks.

BUREAUCRATS AND THE PUBLIC INTEREST

More arguably—but consistent with a major thesis of this book—is a fourth function: the contribution of development managers to the shaping and definition of a "public interest" that in every sector of government may constrain the self-regarding demands of competing interest groups. As career officials in the service of their state and society, and as politicians come and go, development managers are the more permanent stewards or custodians of a public interest that extends beyond the satisfaction of immediate individual or group interests. In Chapter 7, I elaborate the theme of managerial professionalism, which includes, among its ethical imperatives, the conception and the defense of the important, if elusive, concept of a public interest. This is a controversial position, due in part to skepticism about the very notion of an identifiable public interest and about the ability or even the appropriateness of unelected mandarins presuming to participate in its definition and interpretation. I limit myself at this stage to asserting that in addition to their generally recognized instrumental, political, and entrepreneurial roles, development managers are vested with this fourth function that relates to the concept of the public interest (Montgomery 1962).

The performance of these functions produces tensions and conflicts. Political elites expect development managers to be complete and perfect instrumentalists. Even the most self-effacing senior development managers cannot, however, escape their political role, but if they practice it boldly and decisively, they may be accused of usurping the politicians' powers; if they decline to act or refer all such matters to their superiors, they can be accused of timidity or failure of initiative. The safest course for most development managers is to interpret political problems in legal or technical terms, to define and present them in technical language, protecting themselves by finessing any obvious entanglement in political decisions. Thus they search for objective formulas to render automatic such basically political processes as the allocation of public-works projects among competing districts. Although this is a useful defensive tactic, it is only a tactic; it does not subtract from their actual political role. The training of development managers should be such that it relieves them of any self-deception and helps them accept moral responsibility for actions that are essentially political, in that they involve the exercise of discretion, produce differential consequences, and distribute differential advantages and costs to different individuals and segments of society.

I mention here, but do not intend to be detained by, the Marxian notion that senior public managers, as a component of the dominant bourgeoisie, cannot implement such bureaucratic reforms as decentralization because these would reduce their power and thereby undermine the hegemony of the class they represent (Hirschmann 1981). This exercise in deductive logic both oversimplifies Marxian class analysis and is disproved by abundant observable evidence. Senior officials do not necessarily share the perspectives of industrial capitalists or of landed rural elites. They can function as a bureaucratic interest group, but frequently they are segmented and disunited. Senior officials are, moreover, driven by mixed motives—a theme I elaborate in Chapter 7—of which the defense of class privileges may be one, but not their only or even their main concern. For that matter, it is not clear that structural reforms that shift the distribution of class power in society reduce their effective influence. They can and do serve as agents of developmental change.

CRITERIA FOR RECRUITMENT

In the evaluation of public bureaucracies, a number of critical problems have emerged that continue to confront the more stable governments in the West and remain unresolved in most LDCs. In this discussion, I assume the advantages of a career civil service, which provides expertise and continuity to the administration of public affairs and whose members remain in office during good behavior until they reach retirement age. I know of no convincing argument that a modern state can staff its bureaucratic structures by any other method, nor do I know of a single successful modern polity that does not conform to these practices (Mosher 1968). I regard the career civil service concept as a nondebatable necessity for any state whose leaders seriously aspire to promote social and economic development. Within the framework of a career civil service there are a number of variations, alternative practices that, especially at the level of management cadres, can affect the quality of public administration. It is these choices that I examine in the next several paragraphs.

The first of these is the principal criterion for recruitment and selection to permanent or career posts in the civil service. The preferred criterion is merit, based on competitive selection—and subsequent advancement—of the best qualified applicants according to objective tests of aptitude, educational achievement, relevant experience, and job performance. The determination of what standards are most appropriate for specific classes of positions, how to measure them, and how to rank applicants for eventual selection continue to be debated among specialists in public personnel management. The principle of selection and advancement by merit, however defined and measured, is widely accepted on two grounds: It provides the state and the public service with the most qualified applicants, and it chooses among competitors according to objective standards; it serves the goals of both efficiency and fairness.

Yet many regimes in LDCs do not follow this method of selecting or promoting development managers. They rely instead on political criteria, rewarding loyal supporters of the regime and its elites with government posts, such loyalty and support being measured by personal or political allegiance or by kinship and ethnic affiliation. Patronage appointments allow political elites to consolidate their position by forging networks of dependent loyalists whose jobs and living standards depend on the continuing power of their patrons. Loyalty and political service are exchanged for government employment. The conventional justification for this practice is that rulers must be able to trust subordinates to enforce their will and implement their policies with enthusiasm. In the hands of neutrals, so the argument goes, policies will not be carried out with the necessary sympathy and understanding; in the hands of careerists who may prove to be closet enemies, the intentions of political elites may be undermined and even sabotaged. Rulers are often more than willing to sacrifice efficiency for fidelity. In the words of the late Chairman Mao, it is more important that subordinates be red than expert.

The notion of representative bureaucracy needs to be addressed in this context. Since public-service positions provide material rewards and status as well as power to shape policies and distribute resources within society, government bureaucracies, it is argued, especially at managerial levels, should faithfully reflect the diverse interests in society. This is especially important in LDCs where government jobs are extremely attractive, especially to educated men and women, and society may be highly differentiated and segmented along ethnic lines. Thus representative bureaucracy provides a means for managing conflict among ethnic communities by allocating government positions in the military as well as the civilian sectors according to the principle of numerical proportionality. Merit criteria and technical efficiency may thereby be compromised or superseded in the interest of distributional equity and political stability. Within each group, selection may be governed by either merit or patronage criteria. On the problematic side, representative bureaucracy may produce informal ethnic networks in government or in individual agencies that promote the interests of their members and channel the flow of public resources and opportunities to ethnic kinsfolk in defiance of formal allocative criteria and even the intentions of political superiors.

Respect for merit criteria in personnel actions, problematic as it may be to identify and measure, is closely associated with effective administrative performance. Yet governments in Third World countries pursue values other than instrumental efficiency and fairness among individuals. It is naive to expect merit criteria alone to determine recruitment and promotion practices. Merit is likely to be one of several criteria for selection and advancement, respected more for some kinds of positions, for example, engineers, doctors and agronomists, than for others that are technically less demanding. In many lines of work, merit is recognized by the establishment of minimum educational attainments; persons who satisfy the minimum requirements can then be appointed or promoted by patronage methods or representative criteria. Development managers, who are themselves often the products of selection by criteria other than pure merit, must be prepared to evoke good performance from staff members selected by equally flawed criteria.

POLITICAL NEUTRALITY

Civil servants everywhere are expected to be loyal to the state that employs them. But how committed need they be—should they be—to the regime currently in office? Classical Western bureaucrats, loyal to the state and its institutions, faithfully execute its laws; their expertise and advice are available to their political masters, whose policies they implement even when they may disagree with them. Between competing political parties, they are scrupulously neutral; they are required to abstain from partisan political activity. Political neutrality is the price the career civil servant pays for continuity in office, for being acceptable to politically responsible ministers from whatever party or faction temporarily holds office.

The contrary view is that the loyalty of civil servants to the abstract state and its laws and institutions is insufficient; the regime in office is entitled to positive loyalty and enthusiastic commitment. Having faithfully served the previous regime and helped to implement its bad policies, politically neutral civil servants may be suspected of moral indifference, tantamount to passive opposition. Upon winning office by election or by violence, a government, according to this perspective, is entitled to fill key managerial posts in the civil service with unambiguously loyal supporters. Only committed civil servants can be relied on to execute the policies of their political masters with enthusiasm and employ their discretionary powers in ways that protect and strengthen the regime. Better sacrifice some expertise and experience to achieve the advantages of commitment and reliability.

Politicizing the civil service is a certain prescription for mediocre performance, since the main criterion for recruitment and survival in office is political loyalty, rather than ability or performance. Political neutrality does not ensure good performance, but it makes it possible; it allows professional standards to be applied and rewarded. When political criteria prevail, loyalty and influence displace talent and performance as criteria for recruitment and advancement; opportunities to professionalize the civil service are consequently limited. Political neutrality facilitates, though it cannot ensure, effective development management.

GENERALISTS VS. SPECIALISTS

What of the choice between generalist and specialist managers? Should managers emerge from the ranks of professional and program specialists, from public-works engineers, agronomists, doctors, economists, and teachers—persons who would be expected, by experience and additional training, to add managerial and policy skills to their programmatic expertise? Or should managers be recruited and trained to be experts in management, with broad policy and general managerial capabilities, administrative generalists able to apply their skills to any substantive field of activity? Should the more senior ranks of the civil service, those that deal with larger policy and managerial issues, be filled exclusively or mainly from a generalist administrative elite, rather than those whose basic training and experience have been in the specialized professions? European, especially British and French (but also Japanese), practice has favored generalists as an administrative elite, monopolizing senior civil service ranks, from which program specialists are mostly excluded. The U.S. pattern frowns on the notion of an administrative elite and encourages the movement of program specialists, primarily by experience, into managerial roles, including the most senior civil service posts available to career personnel.

My conclusion from observing both these patterns is that each of them is workable, but that the growing complexity of government favors the U.S. pattern, which calls for adding managerial expertise to backgrounds in professional and programmatic specialization. This requires more formal midcareer training in policy analysis and in managerial skills than is generally available to specialists when they advance into managerial roles. Conversely, generalists, whose administrative and policy skills are often more assumed than demonstrated, can be required as they advance in their careers to specialize in broad substantive and policy areas—for example, finance, urban affairs, public works, environmental and resource management—so that they become competent to supervise program specialists. This pattern, however, imposes a ceiling on the career aspirations of engineers, doctors, economists, and other professionals that can seldom be justified by the superior talent, training, and performance of generalists in managerial positions.

Either arrangement can be made to work. The training of generalists in managerial and policy skills can be more explicit, and they can be compelled to specialize in broad program areas; alternatively, program specialists can be required to enhance their managerial skills as they move into administrative roles. Unless, however, there are compelling political reasons to favor the persistence of the generalist-elite system—for example, that the All-India Administrative Service counteracts dangerous centrifugal tendencies in the Indian federal state—the presumption for future development should favor the U.S. pattern, adding managerial skills to a foundation in program specialization. The complexity of modern government puts a premium on substantive knowledge and experience, while the entrenchment of a cadre that claims high status immediately upon recruitment from universities is unfair to specialists who are equally and often better educated and no less talented or experienced in actual managerial tasks.

IMPROVING BUREAUCRATIC PERFORMANCE: CLASSICAL METHODS

How does one improve the performance of bureaucratic organizations charged with the implementation of development programs? During four decades of experience with international assistance, the main donor agencies have employed four methods:

1. Enhancing managerial skills by education and training in the institutions of the donor country and by establishing and strengthening training institutions and programs in LDCs. The main objective has been to upgrade the management skills, the professional orientation, and, more recently, the policy-analytical competence of individual career executives (Kerrigan and Luke 1987).

2. Improving the technologies available to managers, thereby enabling them to use resources more efficiently and make their performance more effective. This transfer-of-technology approach includes financial methods such as budgeting, accounting, and expenditure control; improving the speed and accuracy of information flows, particularly through microcomputers; and more rational methods of scheduling, monitoring, and evaluating program operations (Kiggundu 1989, ch. 6).

3. Rationalizing organization and procedures and adjusting structures and methods to enhance management control, save resources, increase efficiency, and speed the delivery of services—applying to government operations the prescriptions and experiences of the scientific management movement and its technocratic successors in private industry (Rondinelli 1987).

4. Strengthening bureaucracies as social institutions, building institutions in ways that both enhance their internal capabilities and improve their ability to interact productively with their external environment and thus sustain the development activities for which they are responsible (Esman 1972b).

These classical methods of management improvement and development and related concerns with program management have been elaborated in an extensive literature that incorporates the state of the art in contemporary development administration (United Nations 1975, 1978; Brinkerhoff 1990). They apply to all levels of activity, from individual programs and enterprises to economic sectors and even to government as a whole. The utility of and continuing need for these methods are clear, even though they are often promoted dogmatically and make insufficient allowance for adaptability to specific Third World conditions. Except for the institution-building approach, their main limitation is their technocratic orientation, assuming as they do that the underlying political and cultural environment will be receptive to and supportive of such innovations. This has proved to be inadequate to the tasks at hand, failing to address the structural, motivational, and political dimensions of development management.

Beyond the technocratic measures that promise increased efficiency, what is most needed is to loosen the rigidities of classical bureaucratic structures and adapt their operations to the uncertainties, complexities, and societal pluralism that characterize the environments in which they operate. The problem with the aforementioned standard approaches to improving development management is not that they are wrong or unnecessary, but that they are too narrow in their conception. They neglect the pluralism within bureaucratic structures and the incentives that motivate behavior—topics that have been extensively developed in the literature on organizational behavior. They overlook the complexities of the external environment that confront all developmental bureaucracies and the political forces that act on all government agencies and the programs they administer.

How then can the structures, procedures, and operations of government bureaucracies be loosened or adapted to enhance their performance as development organizations? How can the advantages of the bureaucratic method of organization and operation, including the control, discipline, and accountability that are essential to responsible government, be reconciled with the need for flexibility and timely response to differentiated publics in pursuit of developmental goals? This question, fundamental to development management, is the main focus of the rest of this chapter. The methods outlined can be categorized as structural, procedural, motivational, political, and the control of abuses.

STRUCTURAL REFORM

Administrative Deconcentration

A continuing problem of bureaucracy, one that can never be finally re-solved, is the balancing of central control with operating discretion by subordinate staff, especially those in the field at a physical distance from headquarters. The inclination of agency headquarters is to apply strict rules, to preprogram all decisions so that their implementation is reduced to routines, and to require all exceptions to be referred to headquarters for amendments to the rules or for special treatment. In this way, senior politicians and administrators, many of whom feel more comfortable and competent dealing with specific operational cases than with general issues of policy, attempt to assert continuing control over specific problems that arise and thereby counteract centrifugal tendencies resulting from the machinations of local elites and the complicity of field staffs. The inclination of field personnel is to ask for some discretion to interpret general policies and specific rules to accommodate the realities they encounter, realities that result from natural and social heterogeneity or changing conditions that could not have been anticipated when rules were formulated and programs designed. These tensions are inherent in all large and complex organizations.

The determination of which concessions headquarters should be pre-pared to make in favor of timely response to local circumstances and which matters require strict uniformity depends very much on the subject. Policy matters that threaten macropolitical consequences are certain to be reserved to the highest levels of government; matters that are considered more routine can be decentralized and handled as incremental adjustments within field bureaucracies. Financial obligations such as taxes and entitle-ments such as pension payments must be precise and uniform, allowing for little or no managerial discretion. The operation of small irrigation systems, local health clinics, or urban sites and services activities may, on the other hand, benefit greatly from—indeed may require—a measure of on-site managerial discretion. Within the same activity, some matters may require uniform rules, for example, the price of pharmaceuticals in rural health centers, while the operation of these facilities ought to be flexible enough to respond to specific local health problems and the convenience of the public.

The main structural expedient for toning up bureaucratic performance is decentralization in its various forms. Here we are not speaking of the state divesting itself of activities that it has been performing and transferring them to nongovernmental agencies by the processes of privatization and deregulation. These processes and their implications for development management are dealt with in Chapter 5. At this point, I limit myself to the twin processes of administrative deconcentration and institutional devolution of activities that continue to be performed by government (Rondinelli, Nellis, and Cheema 1984; Silverman 1990). This problem arises because of the aforementioned tendency of governments to concentrate decision making in the capital city and at the top reaches of government hierarchies. The consequence is that headquarters is overloaded with small decisions, action is long delayed, decisions are made without significant input of local information or understanding of local circumstances, and subordinate personnel, especially in the field, are deprived of incentives to use their initiative or to respond to the needs and convenience of the public. Bureaucracy thus becomes a cumbersome, inflexible, and unresponsive apparatus.

In Chapter 2, I referred to the societal pluralism and environmental variations that complicate the problems of governance. Rigorously centralized, preprogrammed, and uniform rules cannot accommodate these variations and contingencies in circumstances and needs. The actions of government, the regulations it applies, and the services it seeks to deliver become unresponsive, even irrelevant to local needs and circumstances, wasting the resources of government while failing to come to terms with local conditions. Speedier communications, even when this becomes technically possible, cannot resolve this problem, because communications cannot remedy the limited capacity of headquarters to process expeditiously numerous low-priority matters that converge on it from the field. Correcting these dysfunctions requires structural adjustments, the most important of which is the deconcentration of authority to act within the state's bureaucratic structures.

Deconcentration represents a major administrative reform that most Third World governments have been slow and reluctant to implement. Although it keeps control within the state bureaucracies, it necessitates changes in organizational culture on the part of both superiors and subordinates, resulting in a perceived loss of control among the former and a reduction of the dependency that many of the latter find reassuring and comfortable. Specifically, it threatens a shift of power in favor of bureaucratic subordinates or local elites. It may confront officials in capital cities, enjoying as they do the amenities of metropolitan living plus proximity to political power, with the distasteful prospect of being reposted to provincial locations. It may disrupt comfortable practices that allow interest groups to limit their efforts to senior officials in the capital city.

There are, however, countervailing tendencies. As their confidence and sophistication increase, central government elites may come to recognize that deconcentration need not entail loss of effective control, but rather a substitution of methods that relieve headquarters of routine details and enhance their ability to concentrate on more consequential problems— policy development, financial allocations, performance evaluation, and program adjustments—while using their administrative resources more effectively. Deconcentration also helps adapt development organizations to the need to reconcile the authority of line managers with the parallel authority of staff officers exercising control over financial, legal, and technical matters. Operating managers face the confusing but unavoidable necessity of living with the complexity of several superiors to whom they are simultaneously responsible. This results in "matrix" arrangements, which require operating managers to adjust to the not entirely consistent but nonetheless legitimate requirements of line and staff superiors, abridging in effect the simplistic maxim of unity of command. By shortening lines of communication, deconcentration simplifies these matrix processes of management, loosening formal patterns of hierarchical authority in order to accommodate functional specialization within a single bureaucratic structure (Davis and Lawrence 1977).

Administrative deconcentration cannot be an all or nothing process. Policy choices and budget allocations must remain in headquarters, while operations are passed down within the organization. The more a matter requires uniformity across the country—for example, tax rates, pension entitlements, fertilizer subsidies—the more centralized the locus of decisions and the more rigorous the rules and the procedures. The more politically sensitive the issue, the more headquarters will insist on control and on preprogramming action; the larger the financial commitment, the greater the number of people affected, and the more complex the technology, the more likely that decisions will be reserved for headquarters. But this leaves large areas of government operations that can and should be delegated to subordinate echelons in the hierarchy, closer to the locus of contact with the public.

Administrative deconcentration cannot merely be decreed. Its implications must take account of shifts in power, especially by officials at the center, who may consider themselves to be prospective losers in such structural changes. Central office personnel will resist transfer to the field. Subordinate managers, especially those in the field, must be trained to levels that condition them to accept greater responsibility for decisions. They must be aware not only of policies and rules, but also of their underlying logic and of ongoing revisions and changes so that the discretion they exercise can take account of these strictures and be contained within allowable parameters. Management information systems must be in place to ensure timely and accurate communication of changes in policies and rules, allow field experience to be incorporated into decision processes, and enable headquarters to be aware of what is happening on the ground. Routine reporting systems need to be supplemented by inspections, program evaluations, and other methods of performance review. Incentive arrangements should reward managers who accept responsibility for taking decisions at their level, even though they may make occasional mistakes. The processes of deconcentration may be implemented in stages over several years, more and more discretion being yielded to field staff as they gain experience and headquarters gains confidence in their ability to assume greater responsibility.

As with all social arrangements, administrative deconcentration is never trouble free; tensions between central control and field discretion are never finally resolved. Field personnel may use their discretion unwisely, corruptly, or in discriminatory ways, yielding to local elites, alienating sections of the public, embarrassing their superiors and even the government. When such incidents occur, as inevitably they do, the tendency is to tighten the rules, circumscribe field discretion, and draw future decisions back to headquarters—in effect, to reconcentrate in order to prevent the recurrence of mistakes and abuses. This response succeeds only in restoring the previous unsatisfactory status quo. While attempting to minimize the possibility of such breakdowns, top management must build the competence and confidence of field personnel and improve communications within the organization. It must be willing to risk and cope with occasional management failures as the price of more timely, effective, and responsive service delivery.

Institutional Devolution

A decentralizing reform with more fundamental institutional implications than administrative deconcentration is the devolution of functions to self-governing local authorities or to organized constituencies (Montgomery 1972; Leonard and Marshall 1982; Smith 1985). Central government yields control of certain services to local units selected by and responsible to local publics. It is thereby relieved of some of the financial burden of providing certain services—a significant benefit when central government finances are under severe and chronic stress. Local communities are free to provide services in such volume and in such ways as they are willing to pay for in response to local demand. Financing of such services may involve some funding from the center, sharing costs, or matching local revenues, taking account of local fund-raising capabilities and efforts. Central funding may be contingent on local compliance with centrally determined service standards enforced usually by inspections.

Except for large municipalities, local governments in most developing countries are notably anemic, their financial capabilities severely circumscribed, their personnel ill-qualified, and the range and quality of their services feeble. Central government politicians and senior civil servants are reluctant to strengthen local government or to yield control of public services, even when they are themselves incapable of providing them.

Central politicians fear that autonomous local authorities may become breeding grounds for opposition politicians or strongholds of politicized ethnic minorities. Senior civil servants fear both the diminution of their own power and the erosion of quality standards in the services over which they would lose direct control—often a self-serving claim. Their disinclination to take initiative on this subject is reinforced by the failure of many local authorities to demand greater responsibility and freedom of action, which is often the consequence of traditions of dependency, insufficient self-confidence, unmobilized publics, and especially fear of additional financial burdens. Thus the growing impulse for devolution in most Third World countries originates less in local demand than in the financial predicament of central governments.

Like administrative deconcentration, institutional devolution carries with it several corollaries and prerequisites. The first is to yield enough financial space to local authorities to enable them to raise sufficient revenues by taxation and user charges to pay for additional or expanded services—maintaining local roads, operating clinics, managing markets. Local authorities will do this only if mandated by central government or if the benefits of additional services are perceived by their constituents as justifying the incremental financial burdens. The second prerequisite is to ensure the basic technical and managerial competence of local personnel. The third is to help local lay leaders to understand and perform their supervisory functions.

This loosening of conventional public bureaucracies cannot be achieved by the sudden abandonment of responsibility by the center. The center must be prepared to facilitate the transfer by providing for the training of local staff, allowing reasonable sources of taxation, and implementing workable divisions of labor between central bureaucracies and local authorities. These will differ sector by sector and service by service. Loan funds that help local authorities to finance needed facilities and equipment may promote the process of devolution. For a period of time, the state may have to supervise and audit local finances and help build the institutions of local self-government. The tutelage may then be gradually withdrawn; autonomous local units will have to be allowed to make their own mistakes, live with the consequences, and learn to solve their problems without provoking the reassertion of centralized controls. Central authorities will have to learn to suffer what they regard as unwise or deviant decisions and even to tolerate local political bases for opposition figures if they are to realize the benefits of local resource mobilization and more activated local communities.

Some central government elites may consider this loss of direct control too risky, on both political and programmatic grounds, and persist in circumscribing local autonomy with tight controls. For this reason, bureaucratic deconcentration, which permits state elites to maintain effective control, is more likely than institutional devolution to be the initial route to structural reform in most LDCs.

The Organization of Work

In conventional bureaucracies, work is organized according to the principle of division of labor, combined with increasing differentiation and specification of tasks and responsibilities as one moves downward from headquarters into the operational hierarchies. At the extremities of the hierarchies, individuals occupy jobs whose functions are strictly defined and narrowly circumscribed within the framework of the specialized unit to which they are accountable. The performance of specialized tasks is prescribed by detailed rules and procedures with which staff members are expected to comply. This has proved to be an effective pattern for organizing work in stable environments, capitalizing on specialization and clarity of functions, where the main objective is to turn out standardized products by fixed routines. The negative consequence is rigidity; sluggishness in accommodating local needs, changing conditions, or consumer preferences; and difficulty in communicating and coordinating efforts across the boundaries of specialized hierarchies even in the same organization. The effects of these barriers can be exaggerated, as organization members typically innovate informal methods of bending or circumventing formal rules to overcome structural and procedural rigidities in the common-sense interest of getting the job done. But this is accomplished in spite of, not because of, the formal arrangements that indeed inhibit the flexibility and adaptability required for many services associated with development.

Much attention has been devoted by academic observers and real-world experiments to methods of adapting complex organizations to the requirements of more dynamic and more uncertain task environments (Katz and Kahn 1978; Bennis 1969). Such methods have become one of the reigning fads in the field of management. Among the structural methods that have emerged are multidisciplinary management teams of specialists assembled for particular problem-solving tasks; once the problem has been solved, the team is dissolved, members return to their parent units, and the new ongoing operations are converted to routines by more or less standard patterns of rule-based specialization. Another pattern is to structure work according to the main products or expected outputs of the organization: specialization by process yielding to more integrated product- or output-oriented patterns of management. Top-down standardized rules, procedures, and job descriptions are relaxed or suspended, while employees are encouraged to combine their collective knowledge, work experience, enterprise, and initiative to structure their own work environment and set and enforce standards of performance oriented to results and cost-effective outputs that are satisfactory to the consuming public. Central headquarters establishes the parameters within which such collective initiative and discretion can be practiced, and it provides necessary resources, including technical and managerial assistance, but the ultimate test of organization and process is the ability of the work group to achieve acceptable outputs or results.

The objective of such reforms in the organization of work is to relax the rigidities of classic bureaucratic structures, not to supplant them. Results of such experiments in Third World situations—and indeed, in Western governments—are not conclusive, though the basic idea is highly touted by an important school of management reformers (Peters and Waterman 1984). Releasing the initiative and experience of rank-and-file staff members, orienting performance to results rather than conformity with rules and procedures, and facilitating communication and coordination across organizational lines are important objectives for coping with task environments that are changeable and characterized by considerable uncertainty. In the framework of responsible government, such reforms must, however, be compatible with the maintenance of essential managerial accountability and control not only of results, but of essential procedures as well. Organizational structures and standard procedures may become ends in themselves, displacing output goals, but they are not invariably or necessarily irrational or dispensable. Some government-mandated procedures and routines guarantee members of the public equal access to services; others ensure equity in personnel practices; others require that government purchasing be subject to competitive bidding and that decisions including financial expenditures be properly recorded. These requirements may, however, constrain or retard the accomplishment of organizational outputs or results.

Thus there are inevitable trade-offs. Although some management controls are clearly necessary in government, the direction of change should favor reforms that relax the rigidity of bureaucratic structure and operations and provide greater opportunity for the exercise of staff initiatives. The reorganization of work away from hierarchical specialization and detailed specification of tasks and procedures is one such method. It is associated with parallel reforms, including structural decentralization and participatory management, which are discussed and evaluated in other sections of this chapter.

Paraprofessionals

The conventional practice of most governments has been to provide services entirely through full-time, permanent, and pensionable employees. The effect of this practice has been to overextend government budgets or, alternatively, to limit the outreach of government, especially in rural areas and urban slums. Governments have found that they simply cannot afford the personnel needed to extend agricultural, health, family planning, and urban community services to large, dispersed publics.

The innovation that has emerged is the paraprofessional expedient; local men and women who lack the formal educational qualifications of normal government employees, but are prepared to work, often part time, at wages far below civil service levels (Esman et al. 1980; Esman 1983). They are often selected and partly compensated by local communities and associations and trained by government agencies to perform specific routine tasks that they can handle adequately at a fraction of what government employees would cost. By this device, governments have been able to extend their services at affordable costs, while communities that benefit take some responsibility for providing facilities and nominating and compensating the paraprofessional staff. This method has been outstandingly effective in staffing primary health services and has also been successful in community development, agricultural extension, social forestry, irrigation management, and the provision of services in urban squatter settlements. It seems to be most effective when local associations accept an active role in the selection process and in monitoring performance.

The paraprofessional method is not cost free or trouble free. Government agencies have found that they cannot train paraprofessionals on a one-time basis and then turn them loose to perform. They require continuous backup support from permanent staff to renew and expand training; provide referral service for nonroutine problems; maintain reliable flows of information and supplies, such as medicines; and sustain morale. When backup support is not available, the system falls apart. When the system is maintained, it is a reliable low-cost method of extending public services and even certain kinds of regulations beyond what would be possible by conventional means. Its potential has only begun to be exploited.

REFORM OF PROCEDURES AND METHODS

Loosening the rigidity, improving the performance, and enhancing the responsiveness of bureaucratic organizations can be facilitated by process innovations and changes in methods of operation. Many of these must be specific to individual programs, for example, simplifying paperwork incident to agricultural credit or speeding the public's access to health services. Many of these reforms depend on rationalizing financial management—budgeting, expenditure control, accounting, and purchasing. Since these essentially technical measures have been elaborately documented and assessed in mainline publications in public management, I do not expand on them here (United Nations 1975, 1978; Caiden and Wildavsky 1974). Instead I focus on a set of less familiar procedural reforms that are likely to be productive in the framework of development management.

Information Management

One of the classical problems of management is how to maintain the integrity of information in bureaucratic structures. Information is an indispensable resource for managers in complex organizations, for both operations and accountability, since all coordinated action depends critically on reliable and accurate communication. For development managers especially, two kinds of communication are essential: (1) information about the external environment, including natural conditions; the needs, preferences, and convenience of the publics they are serving; and the activities and intentions of other organizations and of political actors that impinge on their areas of responsibility; and (2) information internal to the organization, especially the general orientation and specific instructions from higher authority, reports of substantive problems and performance from subordinates, and data about conditions within the organization, especially the capabilities, morale, and performance of personnel.

There are four problems with information flows that managers must address but can never entirely solve:

1. Information comes at a cost in time and money; it is never a free good. At the same time, managers cannot cope with, cannot absorb, unlimited flows of data. In order to control costs, ensure the availability of needed data, and exclude extraneous information, management provides routines for information flows, including the preselection of categories of information that enter the standard communications channels. Other classes of information are thereby excluded from routine channels, though they might prove at some time to be important for decision and action.

2. Flows of information in complex, especially bureaucratic, organizations are vulnerable to distortion, willfully or by accident. Policy statements and instructions from senior management, as they trickle down the hierarchy and are successively detailed and refined to apply to specific conditions, can be interpreted to yield guidelines that diverge markedly from original intent. Information flowing from working levels can be screened, aggregated, and presented in ways intended to protect subordinate managers from criticism or provide what it is believed senior management wants to hear (Laudon 1974).

3. Even the availability of accurate and timely information does not ensure that it will be used. Some managers tend to rely on wisdom, intuition, previous experience, restricted but trusted sources, or entirely on routine data. To economize on time and effort, they succeed in excluding or overlooking other kinds of potentially useful information. They may lack the skills, curiosity, or incentives to reach out to alternative sources or even to make good use of information that is within their grasp.

4. In the competition for resources and influence within a single organization or between organizations, information is seldom politically neutral. Availability or denial of information can be a weapon used to promote or defend particular organizational interests. What information is requested and what information is supplied, even when the latter is technically accurate, must frequently be evaluated in political terms: who benefits, who is hurt, and how the information is being employed for political advantage (Dutton and Kraemer 1985).

The loosening of bureaucratic organizations for developmental purposes, particularly decentralized operations, has important implications for the management of information. These include several themes, for example, that routine information flows need to be redesigned to emphasize performance goals and the relative effectiveness of alternative means rather than meticulous compliance with standard procedures. Information about the external environment must be accorded higher priority. Management cannot depend entirely on routine information flows; its antennas must be tuned to multiple sources and channels, both internal and external.

Routine flows of reasonably reliable and timely data can be speeded at moderate cost by such technologies as microcomputers, which also facilitate the storage and retrieval of large volumes of potentially useful materials. Microcomputers are a tangible manifestation of the revolution in informatics that has favorable implications for management and program operations. Although their technical dimensions are beyond the scope of this book, microcomputers' ability to store and retrieve large volumes of data, to communicate information speedily and accurately, can greatly increase the productivity of staff, speed their response time, and adjust responses to specific local needs (United Nations 1988). Their effects on airline reservations and banking transactions are familiar to laypeople in all Western countries. For some kinds of decisions, they facilitate managerial centralization—for example, the regional allocation of scarce medicines; for many others, they foster decentralized operations because of the useful and timely information they make available to decision makers on the ground. The costs of microcomputers are modest and declining; the hardware has become quite robust; reasonably literate staff can be trained to use them.

The association of personnel with such high-technology equipment has positive effects on morale and self-esteem. Provisions for the prompt and competent servicing of such equipment are feasible.

The main difficulty is the generation of software that is relevant to the distinctive natural and institutional environments of individual countries, since these markets are often small and the costs of developing and testing suitable software are consequently high. The software bottleneck is especially difficult for applications that are intended to be used for policy planning, program design, and project management, rather than for routine operations.

Microcomputers can, however, facilitate management in nearly all government operations: from financial accounting to crop reporting, from the control of inventory for medical and health installations to the scheduling of road maintenance. Individual positions and entire operations can be redesigned for enhanced efficiency and responsiveness, though promised cost savings are often slow to materialize. There is, however, one critical condition that must be met before the communications revolution can pay off for developing countries: Information that becomes available must actually be used at all levels of decision making and of action as well; otherwise, microcomputers become expensive toys. Speedy and accurate information facilitates, but cannot ensure, responsive action. Hospital X may communicate an urgent need for penicillin and surgical gloves, but unless the warehouse staff acts promptly and responsively on that information, and unless the supply system has provided the warehouse with these items, information alone will not secure them. Experienced managers recognize that it is easier to move information than to achieve disciplined and responsive action in large organizations; information is a tool, never a substitute, for management.

Routine flows, both quantitative and qualitative, remain the principal informational resource for both operations and accountability. These requirements must, however, be monitored periodically to ensure that headquarters does not overwhelm field offices with requests for series of data that are seldom used—a chronic and valid complaint of working-level staff. Reporting requirements must concentrate on data directly instrumental to programmatic operations and goals, and the means of achieving them. The integrity of routine flows is a constant preoccupation of senior management, which must expend resources to check and verify their reliability.

Although routine flows are essential to orderly management, they are never sufficient, especially in the dynamic context of developmental changes. Since the critical tests for development-oriented programs are their beneficial impacts on the public, baseline information about their underlying circumstances as well as updated reports on the effects of program interventions assume high priority in information flows. To monitor program impacts, managers must supplement routine channels by personal visits, periodic formal and informal inspections, staff conferences, employee suggestions, and complaints and demands from the public, politicians, and interest groups, while maintaining a healthy appreciation for the tendency of suppliers to bias the selection and interpretation of information in their favor. When managers take advantage of multiple channels and demonstrate an openness to nonroutine and nonconventional sources, useful information will flow; otherwise reporting can degenerate into mindless procedures.

Improvements in the communication and uses of management information depend on the skills and the incentives that motivate management personnel. Enhancement of these skills can be achieved as a component of management training, including, but not limited to, the uses of computerized data. These skills cover the responsive uses of routine and repetitive information on current operations as well as the measured investment of effort and time in the identification and acquisition of baseline and other societal data. Incentives to employ data more productively can be linked to improved methods and criteria for bureaucratic accountability. Traditional systems of accountability for the use of inputs, mainly financial, impose very narrow informational requirements. When these are supplemented by performance criteria—how well development outcomes are realized by various programmatic outputs—incentives for managers to search out and use information as a resource for achieving these performance goals are greatly increased. This is especially true when goals are publicized and working-level staff as well as members of the public contribute to the needed exchanges of information.

When development activities are carried out under conditions of such uncertainty that measurable goals cannot readily be specified—for example, in family planning or social forestry—development programs become action hypotheses that must be carefully monitored and evaluated to determine what methods are likely to be effective under specific circumstances (Rondinelli 1983). Information management in such situations tracks and assesses both processes and impacts. Organizational learning and incremental knowledge building require continuous information exchanges between the staff of development agencies and the affected publics.

Social Marketing

One of the most significant process improvements, one that applies to a broad range of government activities that have a direct impact on the public, is incorporated in the concept of social marketing. The underlying notion of social marketing is that service providers should attempt to determine what the public, their prospective "customers," actually want and prefer, what methods of supplying the service they would find most welcome and convenient, and then attempt to satisfy their customers' demands. Instead of unilaterally setting the terms and conditions of public services, government bureaucracies should make a positive effort to adapt them to the expressed needs and preferences of the public. Instead of waiting for the public to claim services, government agencies ought to reach out, attempting actively to "sell" or extend their services. Government agencies would then expect to be evaluated by their success in inducing the public to use the services they provide, adjusting both content and methods to public demand. When government finances limit the scale of services that can be provided, a measure of effective social marketing may be the willingness of the public to cofinance or even to coproduce and coprovide such services by paying user fees or otherwise contributing to their costs (Kotler 1976).

In the conventional bureaucratic model of service delivery, a government agency designs services as authorized by law and the availability of funds and makes them available to the public. The government thus is a passive provider of services, which the public is free to claim or disregard. Social marketing places government in the more proactive role of inducing or persuading potential consumers to avail themselves of services that, in turn, must be made attractive to them. As with commercial marketers, the agency's incentive system must provide rewards, material and nonmaterial, to those who successfully reach and engage their potential customers. One way to do so—the favorite of classical economists and of their contemporary acolytes in the "public choice" school—is to facilitate competition among two or more providers of services.

Even when competition or consumer choice is not feasible, the extension or marketing approach to public services represents a departure from the conventional bureaucratic model. One modest example in agriculture is the one-stop facility in which several related services to farmers that are conventionally supplied at different locations and through separate procedures by specialized agencies, such as extension, credit, seeds, and fertilizer, are made available in integrated packages at a single location to cater to the convenience of farm "customers." Social marketing by government agencies cannot quite attain the goal of consumer sovereignty, but it begins to orient government services decisively in that direction. Its success depends on shifting the patterns of bureaucratic motivation.

MOTIVATIONAL REFORM

Rewards and Punishments

The incentives that apply in bureaucratic organizations often thwart development performance. Advancement is based on patronage or seniority.

Initiatives that fail may be punished, while meticulous adherence to rules and procedures, even at the cost of responsiveness to public needs, exposes the civil servant to little risk. There are few rewards and considerable risk in deviating from prescribed procedures; the integrity of formal rules and procedures displaces the goals of service. Yet it is clear that individual civil servants cannot be left entirely free, on their own unrestrained initiative, to set aside or dispense with organizational rules and routines, especially those that concern finances. Some controls continue to be needed. When, however, the main goal is performance rather than control, there are opportunities to loosen detailed controls and stimulate bureaucratic initiative and responsiveness by shifting the incentive structure that applies to both individuals and groups (Matheson 1978; Lawler 1983).

The effectiveness of incentives and rewards varies with national cultures. Some cultures value individualism, others group solidarity. Some assign a high value to security, others to goal achievement. The specific incentives that are intended to motivate personnel need to be congruent with the realities of their society. It must be recognized, however, that development implies cultural change and cultures are not immutable. Rewards for service-oriented performance can be directed to individuals or to groups. They can be both material—including pay raises, cash bonuses, promotions, and opportunities for self-improvement through training—and nonmaterial—including special symbolic recognition for excellent service. The criteria should be related to performance of the agency's service goals as evaluated both by the public, in terms of their responses to the services, and by bureaucratic superiors.

The danger of applying selective incentives and bonuses is that in the perverse egalitarian ethos of many large organizations, such rewards may soon lose their selectivity and be awarded equally to all, or be regarded as entitlements or routine elements in the compensation structure. One method of dealing with this problem is to emphasize rewards to groups rather than individuals, in ways that comport with cultural norms and avoid the morale-destroying effects of individual competition within a single organizational unit. Another method is the use of performance contracts or understandings that are set by mutual agreement, establish specific goals for organizational units, and provide a reward for achieving these goals, leaving the units considerable latitude for initiative in the methods used.

No such arrangements can ever be foolproof, as staff members may find ways to manipulate information, distort their efforts, and emphasize goals that are easily measured and achieved. The disbursement of funds, for example, is more easily achieved and more easily measured than the achievement of substantive results. The latter, however, should be the principal criterion for evaluating performance and allocating rewards.

Orienting goals and sanctions toward performance, results, or outputs can be a mighty step forward in achieving more than mere compliance with the letter of procedures and routines or the expenditure of bureaucratic effort. The focus on results is especially useful if the public can be involved in the evaluation process. Public involvement can be achieved and assessed indirectly by the public's use of services or their compliance with regulations or directly by periodic evaluation of performance, in which local organizations are induced to participate.

The employment of selective rewards to enhance performance is often thwarted by difficulties in measuring and evaluating organizational outputs. There will always be some tension in bureaucratic organizations between integrity of procedures that are readily measurable and responsiveness to public needs and convenience, which is harder to identify and evaluate. This tension, however, is not a valid reason for failing to emphasize service and output rather than adherence to procedures as the main test of satisfactory performance and the main incentive for career advancement and other rewards.

Working Conditions and Supplies

Poor working conditions are a major disincentive to performance, a problem that particularly affects field staffs in Third World countries. As one moves from the national capital to provincial centers and then to outlying areas, working conditions tend to deteriorate, facilities and equipment are less modern and often out of order, and the flow of supplies needed for program operations tends to be less reliable. Field personnel who deliver services to the public often work in cramped, dingy, poorly lighted and even unsanitary quarters, with antiquated office and filing equipment. Their vehicles and machinery are often out of commission for lack of maintenance and replacement parts; their gasoline allotments are insufficient to enable them to reach their public; the flow of supplies such as cement, spare parts, medicines, fertilizer, and textbooks is frequently delayed or unavailable for extended periods; and their requests for assistance are often ignored. They feel, often correctly, that they are at the end of the line in dead-end jobs. The resulting sense of isolation, neglect, helplessness, and cynicism that is so common among field personnel saps morale and undermines performance. Low job satisfaction produces low productivity and unresponsive performance; low productivity alienates the public; alienated publics reinforce low job satisfaction in a vicious circle of organizational decay (Smith 1967; Esman 1983).

Although these conditions have been exacerbated by the financial strains that have confronted many governments during the past decade, they were present even in better times. The underlying problem is the inability of the public to press their demands on officialdom. The symptoms are the preoccupation of headquarters staff with their own working arrangements, the low priority they attach to the working conditions of field personnel, and their failure to establish and maintain reliable lines of communication and supply with field offices. Even when shortages and delays are unavoidable, careful allocation and timely notification enable field units to plan and to improvise, to make the best use of limited means. This also helps reassure field personnel that they have not been abandoned and that their efforts continue to be appreciated.

The success of development programs hinges on the performance of field staffs, on those who are actually in contact with the public—a reality that is often overlooked. Therefore, the disincentives and depressing effects of poor working conditions and unreliable flows of supplies are a serious problem for development managers. There should be realistic possibilities of career advancement to stimulate and reward ambitious employees. Sustaining the morale of field personnel should be a continuous preoccupation of development managers at all levels. Positive measures to improve working conditions, even incrementally and in small ways, can help. Establishing systems for advance notification of the availability of supplies and prompt shipment when they become available can enable field staff to live with shortages and disappointed publics. If workable systems are in place, scarcities can be managed. This assumes, however, a continuing concern for the working arrangements of field staff and for the modest incentives that enable them to maintain their self-esteem and to perform even under difficult conditions.

Participatory Management

An underutilized motivator of bureaucratic performance is incorporated in the concept of participatory management. Without abridging the hierarchical authority structures that define bureaucracy, participatory management institutionalizes the regular and systematic consultation of staff members at all levels. It encourages and rewards the contribution of relevant and otherwise unobtainable information and experience toward solving the ground-level problems that all organizations encounter and beyond that toward improving the methods and timing of agency action. This process may be a major stimulus to motivation as it enhances the self-esteem of staff members and raises their status from mere instruments of the will of others to respected sources of information and shapers of action. It can enhance performance at low cost. The benefits of this change in organizational culture can, however, be realized only if the process proves to be consequential, to demonstrate to front-line managers and employees that their initiatives have discernible impacts on what the agency does, that it is more than a symbolic, token, or formalistic exercise.

In authoritarian societies where subordinates are expected to defer to status superiors, participatory management may appear to threaten the status and power of managers. They may resist it as a time waster, a generator of needless conflict, an ill-conceived concession to naive populism, or a mischievous challenge to their legitimate hierarchical authority. Subordinates, long accustomed to meticulous compliance with rules and procedures, may feel uncomfortable or that they are being asked to take unnecessary risks in volunteering proposals to change methods that have been legitimatized by long practice and sanctioned by their superiors. That participatory management has the potential for evoking information and ideas that can materially improve the performance of bureaucratic organizations in terms of more efficient resource use and greater responsiveness to the public is, however, amply demonstrated in a rapidly growing literature drawn from concrete experience (Lawler 1988).

That participatory management involves significant behavioral change among both managers and staff is equally clear. Like any social innovation or institutional change, it has to be deliberately introduced by senior management, fostered over extended periods of time, featured in training programs, and emphasized in reward structures. It is, however, among the more useful potential motivators available for Third World bureaucracies. More than any other method, it can enhance staff morale while promoting and sustaining organizational learning, the process by which an organization at all levels builds and adapts its knowledge base in relation to both its internal dynamics and the publics it serves.

Like most reforms, however, participatory management can be oversold. Aside from the enhancement of staff morale, its principal contributions to program effectiveness and to instrumental efficiency are likely to be felt at the level of operations and at the interface between front-line management and the public, where their experience can evoke alternatives to prevailing methods and rules. While sponsoring and encouraging such initiatives, senior management remains responsible for evaluating the effects of proposed improvements on the policies and practices of the organization that may not be obvious to working-level staff, recognizing also that the latter may be promoting their own agendas and interests that may not be entirely congruent with those of the organization. Fresh perspectives on the organization and its mission, policy innovations, and their implementation are more likely to be generated by senior management and "sold" to operating-level staff. In this case, participatory processes are useful in speeding the adoption of changes, reducing the accompanying frictions, identifying unanticipated obstacles, and especially adapting changes to working-level realities. Participatory processes can be beneficial both in motivating staff and in improving operations as an adjunct to, but not a substitute for, managerial initiatives and responsibilities.

Civil Service Compensation

As a problem in motivation, the compensation levels of civil servants cannot be avoided. During the immediate postcolonial period, civil service salaries generally provided a relatively secure and dignified standard of living at all levels of the hierarchy, with the promise of an adequate pension upon retirement. Especially for professionals and members of the administrative elite, whose positions had been held mainly by colonial expatriates, salaries and perquisites such as housing and transportation were very generous by local standards, providing incumbents with comfortable middle-class life-styles. The years since independence have witnessed in most developing countries the progressive erosion of the real compensation of civil servants as inflation and chronic fiscal stringency have eaten away at real salaries. Multiplication of the numbers of government employees for reasons of patronage or as antidotes to the political risks of educated unemployment has put further pressure on salary scales. As a consequence, in many Third World countries civil service salaries at all levels are now insufficient to support families. Those who can, abandon their positions to join the private sector or to emigrate; those who remain must often supplement their salaries by engaging in corrupt practices, moonlighting in second and third jobs, or drawing on private or family resources. Salary differentials between senior posts and rank-and-file positions have been sharply compressed.

The consequence has been demoralization, loss of status and self-esteem, and inability or disinclination to concentrate on official responsibilities, not to mention efforts to be responsive to the public (Klitgaard 1989). Although the stress is more intense in some countries than in others, the problem is sufficiently pervasive to constitute a general threat to the ability of governments to manage developmental services. States, such as Malaysia, whose governments have demonstrated the ability and willingness to maintain the real value of civil service compensation, continue to be rewarded by relatively competent, faithful, and honest performance. In other states such as Nepal and Ghana, which have been unable to do so, public services have virtually collapsed, and those that remain are riddled with corruption and malfeasance. Material compensation alone may not be enough to motivate competent, devoted, and responsive performance, but the impoverishment of civil servants almost certainly destroys all incentives.

Rectifying this impasse produces multiple dilemmas. Restoring economic growth and implementing more effective tax regimes are essential but obviously not easy. Privatization and deregulation reduce the need, at least on the margin, for government services, but discharging redundant staff increases unemployment and suffering and, at least in the short run, political alienation. Restoring salary differentials that recognize and reward greater responsibilities may help to retain and remotivate professional and managerial personnel, but the latter cannot perform if subordinate staff continue to feel that their essential livelihoods have not been attended to.

Even in states where the salary crunch has not assumed crisis proportions, inadequate financial compensation drains the morale of civil servants and limits their commitment to the minimum that the job requires. Motivational measures such as participatory management, better training, more adequate facilities, better working conditions, and nonmaterial recognition and rewards are important supplements, but they cannot serve as substitutes for fair salaries and reasonable material compensation. Development mangement may be hostage in many countries to the primordial task of salary rectification to the minimum threshold that permits civil servants to meet the basic material needs of their families. Only at that point can other incentives that promote excellence and responsiveness be brought into play.

POLITICAL PRESSURES:
RESPONSIVENESS AND ACCOUNTABILITY

In the conventional theory and standard practice of bureaucracy, accountability runs exclusively to hierarchical superiors. The preferences of the various publics are presumably expressed and reflected through conventional political processes, which eventually reach government elites and may result in revised laws, policies, or administrative rules. Alternatively, information flowing through bureaucratic channels may achieve similar results. In practice, those at all levels who can mobilize political clout may attempt to penetrate bureaucratic structures in order to influence behavior and outputs in directions beneficial to them. Political pressure at the level of program implementation is generally considered in bureaucratic circles to be illegitimate, "political interference" that most career officials resent and deplore as compromising legal and objective standards in decision making, impairing the integrity of hierarchical authority, and undermining the basic bureaucratic ethos of accountability upward.

In the authoritarian political systems that prevail in most LDCs, where the publics are politically demobilized and relatively powerless, the ethos and practice of upward accountability effectively strip them of significant influence over the behavior or the outputs of bureaucratic agencies. The result is also a loss in efficiency, since officials whose accountability is only upward are inclined to respect the uniformity of rules and standard procedures rather than adapting their efforts and outputs to the specific conditions and preferences, not to mention the convenience, of their publics. One of the objectives of development management must be to achieve greater responsiveness by bureaucratic actors to their diverse publics, to constrain the dominant theme of accountability upward with the necessity of responsiveness downward.

Such responsiveness is most likely to be realized when the publics have the capacity to articulate their interests, when they are organized formally or informally into associations that empower them to express their collective demands, to engage in some patterns of exchange with suppliers of services (Esman and Uphoff 1984). There is no dearth of grassroots associations in developing countries, but their activities are limited by concerns on the part of state elites that autonomous associations might challenge their political control or, like local authorities, provide political bases for oppositional or even subversive forces. Most such associations, however, tend to be apolitical and pose no real threat to state elites; many rulers have gained increased confidence in their ability to maintain their grip on power; and fiscal stringency compels governments to look for alternative or complementary sources of resource mobilization and to enhance the efficiency of the resources they commit to public services. The latter requires greater responsiveness to specific publics and this, in turn, necessitates a shift in bureaucratic accountability to include the relevant public as well as hierarchical superiors.

The themes of dual accountability and optimal responsiveness cannot be treated simplistically. Both concepts involve internal tensions. Responsiveness to publics involves a beneficial change in emphasis in the direction of instrumental efficiency and consumer satisfaction, and it sets the preconditions for the realization of coproduction, a concept that is elaborated in Chapter 6. Responsiveness, however, can seldom if ever be complete or categorical. Some demands from some elements in the public may be so unreasonable, so self-regarding, indeed so contrary to law and policy as to be totally unacceptable—to be heard but not heeded. Moreover, there are necessary boundaries, varying from program to program, that must constrain the ability of field-level staff to modify rules and procedures in the interest of responsiveness and satisfying consumer demand. For these reasons, the concept of optimal responsiveness is appropriate; this means greater responsiveness than is now practiced or permitted in most bureaucracies, but responsiveness that is limited by the legitimate requirements of systemwide equity and responsibility.

Similarly, accountability—the sense of whom subordinate officials must satisfy—can be neither entirely upward nor entirely downward. The goals of development administration require that government servants feel a much greater obligation than in the past to satisfy the public, and that evidence of the practice of this kind of accountability should become an important criterion in evaluating their performance. But this must be consistent with the continuing and simultaneous imperative of upward accountability, which is essential to the integrity of responsible government. Such tensions or competing pressures are common in human affairs and can never be eliminated or entirely resolved. The loosening of bureaucratic structures in most LDCs, however, requires significant movement in the direction of greater responsiveness and accountability by civil servants to the publics they are committed to serve. Combined with participatory management, responsiveness downward to public demand represents a far-reaching reform in public management.

CONTROL OF ABUSES

The main abuses associated with Third World bureaucracies are corruption, negligence, and arbitrary behavior, all of which victimize the public and compromise the effectiveness of development management. Corruption usually involves the selling of public services or preferential access to public services that should be awarded according to objective criteria, free of what economists euphemistically designate as "rents" or unearned income (Scott 1972; Nicholson and Connerley 1989). In many countries and in many departments, official corruption has become institutionalized, a predictable element in transactions between the public and government personnel. Often justified in terms of low civil service salaries, it has the effect of diverting resources for the benefit of civil servants and their political patrons while taxing the public and undermining respect for government.

Negligence, on the other hand, is a consequence of nonfeasance by officials, depriving the public of services to which they are legally entitled; in effect, the withering of bureaucratic discipline as civil servants attend to their own interests and convenience rather than those of the public. Negligence or nonfeasance may also be explained by shortages of supplies or failure of government to provide transport.

The related abuse of arbitrariness can be defined as the treatment of the public by procedures that are unpredictable, vary over time, or discriminate among individuals and groups.

These abusive forms of behavior are partly the consequence of failures to exercise managerial control; they also reflect the penetration into bureaucratic ranks of norms from the surrounding society, such as obligations to kinsfolk that make more effective claims on the behavior of civil servants than the formal rules of office. These can explain but never justify the abuses. Minimizing their incidence is a compelling requirement of development management. One such method is to reduce the secrecy and increase the transparency of government transactions, especially in the financial realm. Capitalizing on this transparency—on the increased availability of information and the openness of transactions—requires an activated public, a function that can be performed by the networks of local associations that I have already mentioned. Empowered by self-organization, public opinion can help to hold civil servants to acceptable standards of behavior. The same can be said for government audits, an expression of top-down control. However, the fear of audits can be effective only if they are relatively speedy and public and if officials understand that audit information will be followed up by action that might jeopardize their careers. Control of the bureaucratic abuses that are endemic in Third World countries requires combined pressures and sanctions from above and from below. These can be strengthened by journalism, which is free enough and courageous enough to expose and attack instances of bureaucratic abuse.

The internalization of professional norms can be a major inhibitor to abusive behavior, a theme that is examined at some length in Chapter 7. None of these methods alone is likely to be effective. The control of these pervasive abuses is a serious and continuing challenge to development management because they entail the demoralization of public services, the failure of discipline, the waste of resources, and the consequent alienation of the public. Cynical acquiescence in such abuses because they "lubricate" and speed official transactions, or because they represent human nature, or because they inhere in the cultures of less developed societies only confirms the perverse suspicion that Third World governments—"soft states"—are inherently corrupt and cannot contribute to economic and social development (Myrdal 1968). Principled management can limit these abuses, but only if it is prepared to confront them directly.

Some students of development administration have been so alarmed by the pervasiveness of bureaucratic abuses, ranging from corruption and arbitrariness to the self-regarding employment of political power, that they advise against any enhancement of bureaucratic capabilities lest these increased capacities only exacerbate the abusive behavior and degenerate into uncontrolled bureaucratic politics (Riggs 1963). Accordingly, they urge that priority be assigned to strengthening the legal and political institutions that control bureaucracies before investing resources in strengthening them. The mainline position in this controversy, one that I have consistently supported, has argued that economic and social development depends critically on building the capacities of governments to produce and provide essential services. Although this emphasizes—but is not limited to—the need to strengthen the organizational capacities of the state and its agencies, it does not ipso facto diminish the importance of simultaneously controlling the political and operational abuses to which public bureaucracies are vulnerable. Thus the legal-political institutions and the bureaucratic institutions of government both need strengthening; the capacities of the state in the face of imperative needs cannot be allowed to languish because of fears that they may be abused pending the viability of mechanisms of control. But warnings about the dangers of abuse ought to be taken seriously; measures of control ought to be promoted lest public bureaucracies victimize the societies they are designed to serve.

MANAGING CONTINGENCIES

Many social scientists are hostile to bureaucracy, especially to state bureaucracy, for a variety of reasons: because it distorts market processes; because it wields arbitrary power; because hierarchical authority relationships compromise human dignity, block information flows, and demotivate creative job performance; because self-regarding bureaucratic power distorts policy goals and exploits the public. Not satisfied merely to condemn bureaucracy, a number of observers have written epitaphs on bureaucracy as a form of human organization, for government as well as industry. But despite such predictions, many of which are expressions of wish fulfillment, bureaucracy has demonstrated remarkable robustness and resilience, nowhere more evident than in the governments of developing countries. The reasons are that (1) bureaucracy provides a form of organization that permits reasonably disciplined control by state elites of complex and large-scale activities over time and extended space and (2) no feasible substitute has been found. It is therefore likely to persist and to remain the organizational environment in which development managers must function.

Like all human institutions, bureaucracy entails many problems, some of which thwart and become impediments to social and economic development. By experience and by the intellectual contributions of many social scientists, means have been innovated to compensate for the dysfunctions and vulnerabilities of bureaucratic organization so that, in the hands of competent and committed development managers, such structures can continue to be instrumental to social and economic development.

The principal methods for adapting bureaucratic organization to developmental tasks have been outlined in this chapter. They include the enhancement of performance orientation, with an emphasis on responsiveness to public demand, implemented by individual and group incentives and rewards calibrated to the realization of programmatic goals. By structural changes such as administrative deconcentration, by process innovations such as social marketing and improved information flows, and by the powerful motivational patterns inherent in participatory management, organizational norms and priorities can shift from mindless compliance with procedures and control of inputs to the achievement of programmatic goals, which, in turn, takes explicitly into account the needs and preferences of the concerned publics. When possible, the publics should be induced to coproduce services and contribute information, material support, and managerial energies to activities from which they benefit. This shift in emphasis stimulates organizational learning—the consequence of freer flows of information within the organization and between the organization and its publics; organizational learning contributes, in turn, to reduction of the uncertainties that are inherent in all development programs.

"Contingency theory," which has recently emerged, argues that the structure of organizations and the procedures they employ must be adapted to the natural and social environments in which services are provided and must take account of the technologies employed. The operation of an airline requires highly centralized management and adherence to standardized procedures that are rigorously enforced; an urban sites and services project should, on the other hand, be flexible and adaptable to local conditions. This very sensible approach to organizational choice places organizations on a continuum between two poles: the "mechanical," which conforms in its essentials to the hierarchical, rule-bound service-delivery model, and the "organic," which emphasizes flexible patterns, participation, horizontal communication, and openness to public demands and preferences (Hage and Finsterbusch 1987). In this scheme, the environment of government requires that its service-providing agencies be closer to the mechanical pole and remain bureaucratic in their structure, but they should nevertheless be able to temper bureaucratic rigidities, as technologies and environmental conditions permit, by decentralization, participatory processes, horizontal exchanges, and openness to the influence of publics and their associations. Nongovernment organizations are more likely to be located on the organic side of the continuum because they are less constrained than government organizations by the imperatives of control and accountability. These findings, emphasizing as they do environmental and technological contingencies, confirm the likelihood that government services must continue to be provided through bureaucratic channels and processes, which, however, can be relaxed to accommodate heterogeneous environments and technological constraints by such methods as have been outlined in this chapter.

Development managers need not take sides in the classical debate among organization theorists between the rationalists and the incrementalists. The former, in the tradition of scientific management, hold that administrative operations should be designed, planned, and controlled from above in order to maximize efficient goal achievement at minimal cost (Gulick and Urwick 1954). The latter argue that imperfect information and unanticipated changes are certain to defy the planners, that management can best be conceived as a process of coping through incremental and sequential adjustments, and that intuition and educated judgment tend to be more reliable tools of management than rigorous design and tight controls (Mintzberg 1973). Any form of purposeful collective action must, however, involve some rational effort to specify objectives, relate limited means to these objectives, schedule the deployment of means over time and space, and evaluate results. The attempt to impose such elemental rationality on program operations is basic to the managerial function. But because uncertainties, turbulence, and contingencies are inherent in the environment of development managers, they must frequently look beyond plans and schedules, rules and precedents, to pragmatic expedients and educated judgment. Since circumstances determine which approach or combination of approaches is appropriate, development managers must be equipped to employ rational methods where possible, judgmental expedients where necessary, and organizational learning at all times.

Structural and procedural reforms can make a significant difference in adapting bureaucratic organizations to developmental tasks, but their implementation is not guaranteed. Although bureaucracy remains the basic organizational framework for development management, the individual agency of government has ceased to be an adequate context for the exertions of most development managers. The reasons for this are the growing complexity of government and the proliferation of functionally specialized activities. Since each of the latter is contained within a separate bureaucratic structure, it becomes impossible for development managers to discharge their programmatic responsibilities without taking into account and coming to terms with parallel governmental entities (Aldrich 1979). To do their jobs adequately, development managers must master their own organizations, but they can no longer so limit their scope. External relationships assume imperative claims on their time, energies, and political skills. We turn to the growing challenges of interbureaucratic interactions in the next chapter.

4

INTERBUREAUCRATIC INTERDEPENDENCY IN THE PUBLIC SECTOR

PEOPLE TEND TO BE MOST CONTENT WHEN THEY WORK UNDER CONDITIONS OF structual simplicity, where relationships are unambiguous, tasks are clearly defined, performance standards are stipulated, and the working environment is free of conflicting pressures. When such conditions do not prevail, individuals often seek to create them by excluding from their consciousness the factors that produce complexity, ambiguity, and uncertainty in their task environment.

There is no such simplicity or certainty in the working environment of development managers. Their world is complicated by competing goals and limited means; the logical nexus between means and ends may be vitiated by legal strictures, political exigencies, uncooperative publics, or the perverse behavior of parallel bureaucratic entities. This is a world of moral ambiguity and organizational complexity; while managers may attempt to simplify it, they must learn to tolerate it in order to cope. For development managers, the most straightforward working environment is implicit in the model presented in Chapter 3, the single bureaucratic organization with unambiguous goals, in total control of a single operating program, endowed inside its boundaries with all the resources it needs to design and implement its mission. There is enough complexity even under these conditions to challenge the most resourceful manager.

Yet the tightly bounded government organization in full control of a program is, in fact, a vanishing species. Though the single-agency perspective continues to dominate teaching and writing in public administration, many government- sponsored policies, programs, and projects overlap the boundaries of a single functionally specialized bureaucratic agency (O'Toole 1985). Their design and especially their implementation may require the participation of two or more agencies (Hanf and Scharpf 1978). The normal tendency of bureaucratic organizations, however, is to maximize self-

74

sufficiency; mimimize dependence on outsiders; defend and, when possible, expand their organizational and substantive boundaries; concentrate on their distinctive programmatic tasks; and cooperate with outsiders only on terms that they find suitable. When programmatic overlapping is unavoidable, various formal patterns of coordination may be mandated by law or government policy, and expedient machinery may be established. The concrete arrangements, however, including exchanges of information, coordinated resource contributions, and compatible operating schedules, are worked out by representatives of the participating agencies or by facilitators specially assigned to that task. Though politicians and interest groups may have access to these negotiations, in most Third World situations such access is problematical; interagency negotiations, operations, and monitoring tend to be handled by civil servants.

More frequently, the need for interagency cooperation is neither visualized in laws nor provided for in government policy. It arises spontaneously from operating necessity. Managers find that the lines of bureaucratic responsibility based on functional specialization do not allow them to be self-sufficient in the execution of their programs. Conditions outside their control compel them to reach out and seek accommodation with other entities, to forge linkages that ensure the complementary resources they need or that respond to external demands for their skills and services.

The interagency dimensions of management entered the literature on organizational behavior and public administration rather late in the development of these fields of inquiry. The dominant focus remains the internal task environment of the individual organization, enterprise, or program, in part because such simplification facilitates the elaboration both of theory and of technologies that foster instrumental efficiency. Although some scholars directing their attention during the past two decades to interorganizational processes and their implications for management have produced useful insights, this remains a minor theme in the literature. On the other hand, the prominence of economic policy measures under recent structural adjustment reforms has begun to focus attention on multiorganizational involvement in the implementation of such policy changes and on the responsibilities of development managers as orchestrators of multiagency coordination rather than as operators of discrete programs in a single organization (White 1990).

In this chapter, I focus on interdependencies among government entities, bureaus within the same department or ministry, organizationally separate departments and parastatals, constitutionally federal structures, and foreign assistance relationships. I address the differences between formal and nonformal and between strong and weak coordinating arrangements. These concrete variations notwithstanding, the logic of interorganizational processes and linkages is remarkably consistent, especially in its implications for the role of senior development managers. Chapters 5 and 6 extend this analysis to include emergent linkages between government agencies and complementary associations and institutions in society.

STRUCTURAL COMPLEXITY AND INTERDEPENDENCY

Within a Single Bureaucratic Organization

Let us begin with the elements of complexity within an individual bureaucratic entity. In Chapter 3, I refer to the inherent tensions between line managers responsible for enforcing regulations or delivering services and specialized staff officers in charge of rules and standards affecting technical, legal, financial, and personnel matters. These internal regulations, imposed by legislation or by senior management, are often perceived by line managers—those responsible for program operations—as onerous, even irrational constraints on their professional judgment and freedom of action; but though they can be resisted and sometimes circumvented, they cannot be easily disregarded or evaded. Tensions between line management and technical supervision and control are regulated by what have come to be known as matrix processes (Davis and Lawrence 1977). An operating manager in a complex organization finds that he must take instructions from and be effectively accountable to several bosses: to a functional supervisor for the maintenance of technical standards, to a financial officer for compliance with expenditure regulations, and to a line superior. When these various instructions are seen to be mutually inconsistent or to impede the performance of operating responsibilities, the operating manager may bargain for relief with the relevant functional specialist or appeal to his line superior to fight the battle on his behalf. The manager is likely to discover that his line superior is willing and able to support him only on a limited number of issues. For the most part, he is on his own to comply or bargain with functional specialists within his own bureaucratic agency for the best deals he can negotiate.

However specific issues of this kind happen to be resolved, the fundamental reality is that managers even in a single organization must live with considerable tension and complexity, responsible simultaneously to several hierarchical superiors, depending on the topic. The hallowed administrative proverb of unity of command simply does not apply. The individual manager must, in fact, absorb and attempt to reconcile binding instructions from multiple sources of bureaucratically legitimate authority. This is the basic reality behind the compelling concept of matrix organization.

A second element of complexity is the tension between functional specialization and territorial integration within a single multifunctional agency.

An example is a department of agriculture that provides crop, forestry, and livestock programs through research, extension, credit, crop and animal protection, and marketing services, each of them implemented by a functionally specialized bureau that maintains tight boundaries, attempts to control all the resources needed to carry out its program, and insists on direct contact with the public. That same department may simultaneously be organized according to the territorial principle, setting up regional offices to coordinate its various specialized field programs as they affect the public.

These two principles of organization, the functional and the territorial, are certain to confront development managers with complexity and conflict. When the functional principle dominates, as it does in most bureaucratic organizations, members of the public may be buffeted by patterns of service that are rational to the separate functional bureaus but are confusing, inconsistent, and even unworkable for the public. Department management may therefore impose a layer of administration with jurisdiction over a defined territory. The regional office is mandated to coordinate the separate functional units in order to increase joint operating efficiency and achieve an integrated pattern of services for farmers in the area. The authority of territorial managers is usually limited, however, since they control neither budgets nor careers nor operating programs, which remain in the hands of the functional bureaus. Managers in the field must learn to be responsive both to their functional-professional chiefs, who control their budgets and careers, and to the territorial director, who is usually senior to them in rank, may be authorized to review their budget requests and write their annual performance appraisals, and has the legitimate task of coordinating within a territory the efforts of several specialized bureaus on behalf of their joint local clientele and of the department.

This classic example of complexity in public administration is likely to confront many development managers. They must live with two or more bosses to whom they are accountable for particular dimensions of their activities; as between territorial and functional patterns of authority and accountability, the lines are often unclear and even conflicting. The tattered formula that managers are responsible on technical matters to their functional bureaus and on operating matters to their line managers produces more ambiguity than clarity. Field managers must attempt to reconcile competing sources of authority—all of them legitimate—and accommodate them, while delivering the service for which they are responsible. Even within a single bureaucratic entity, especially one that operates over considerable space and engages dispersed publics, complexity, ambiguity, and tension are the lot of the development manager. The director of a department responsible for community health services must stretch meager resources over competing needs for health education, environmental sanitation, and primary care; these activities that have taken weeks of effort to justify for budgetary purposes may be abruptly interrupted by an epidemic in a particular region or even overwhelmed by a disaster such as AIDS; these produce irresistible pressures to shift priorities, necessitating a complex set of operational adjustments that are likely, however, to generate more public complaints and internal tension than satisfaction. Rules and precedents for dealing with such competing pressures are usually of limited help; they can seldom be reduced to routines. The task of coping depends on the manager's judgment of what is feasible under the circumstances.

Interdepartmental or Horizontal Interdependency

The competence of government bureaucracies—their legal authority, their financing, the skills and outlook of their senior staff—tends to be defined along functional lines. A ministry of agriculture is not likely to be involved in managing hospitals, nor a ministry of health in building roads. Bureaucratic agencies are inclined to defend their functional turf against encroachment or threats of encroachment by potential competitors and to reach out for new activities when opportunity beckons. Familiar jurisdictional disputes recur: Should agricultural universities be controlled by the ministry of education or of agriculture? Should the electricity parastatal have the capacity to build its own power stations, or should all construction be centralized in the ministry of public works? Bureaucrats are conditioned to look upward in their functional hierarchies for guidance and support and to eschew lateral communication or coordination of operations with parallel bureaucracies.

Whatever the origins or criteria for functional allocations among ministries, departments, and parastatal agencies, however, the critical reality is that development managers are seldom if ever in a position to control all the resources they need to accomplish their programmatic goals. Much as they would prefer to look only inward, to be able to control and deploy all the resources they need within their own organizations, they are frequently compelled to look outward, to claim resources, services, and assistance from organizations they do not control. They, in turn, may find themselves importuned by outsiders to provide services that they control, which may be incidental to or even a distraction from their main responsibilities, but are necessary to the mission of another organization.

Here I refer not to the obvious dependency of all operating agencies on what may appear to them to be the arbitrary and fickle moods of a ministry of finance, but to the necessary sets of linkages that evolve because of functional interdependencies among the various agencies of government. Some may be regulated by well-defined routines—the ministry of health tests the water supply, which is managed by public works; the electricity corporation provides the power needed to operate irrigation pumps controlled by the ministry of agriculture. Other such arrangements may be ad hoc: Public works is requested to make repairs on a hospital operated by the ministry of health; the welfare ministry asks the ministry of agriculture or the food corporation to release food for victims of a flood emergency and the ministry of transport to provide the vehicles and arrange the shipments.

Because they are not hierarchical, these external or horizontal relationships must be managed outside normal bureaucratic channels and patterns. Command styles and supervisory practices must be supplanted by diplomatic styles and negotiating skills in these expressions of interbureaucratic politics. The bargaining resources of the parties are likely to be unequal and to influence the negotiating processes and the outcomes of individual transactions. When a producer of goods or services must cajole or persuade another government agency to accept its output—for example, when a ministry of education must persuade a ministry of agriculture to employ the graduates of its universities—the supplier may have to adapt its output to the preferences of the user; the opposite may be the case for a monopoly supplier such as the electric power corporation, where the user has no alternative. When, on the other hand, a claimant for services is dependent on the goodwill of a supplier, when public works is requested to build access roads for a new land-development scheme, the terms of trade favor the supplier's priorities and convenience. When the consumer of interdepartmental transactions has funds to purchase needed services, the consumer's bargaining power increases, and negotiations may hinge primarily on price. When needed services are uncompensated, included only in the general obligations of the bureaucratic supplier and financed by the supplier's budget, then the claimant may have to wait in line and will have relatively little influence over the process or the product.

Among bureaus within a single department and among departments within a single ministry, functional interdependencies and exchanges are not uncommon. Where feasible, departments will attempt to be self-sufficient at some cost to efficiency, as when a livestock department attempts to grow its own forage rather than rely on the agronomists employed by the department of agriculture. Within a single ministry, these relationships may conflict, but they can be regulated and facilitated by a common bureaucratic authority. Even then, pluralism within ministries usually leaves the working out of specific relationships to the political skills of line managers. Between ministries, formal integrating arrangements are available only on matters that are critical enough to reach the highest levels of government; terms of settlement are expressed only in general language, which must then be interpreted by the competing parties.

The arrangements that ensue in these interdepartmental exchanges reflect the ability of managers at all levels to negotiate terms that take account of the political and material resources available to them and their bargaining

skills. Coordination may be needed for program development and evaluation as well as for operations; monitoring, negotiating, and adjusting
represent continuing claims on the energies and time of development
managers. These problem-solving relationships may be inhibited by procedural rigidities, scheduling conflicts, competing claims on resources, and
even by issues of protocol—the relative social status, educational attain-
ment, or bureaucratic position of the managers involved in such transagency
linkages. They may, on the other hand, be fostered by informal ties of
friendship resulting from common educational and training experiences,
previous service together, or extended kinship or neighborhood origins
that promote interpersonal trust and facilitate communication.

Interjurisdictional or Vertical Interdependency: Federal Systems

Some Third World states are federal in their structure. Some functions are
assigned to the central government, while regional or provincial authorities
are vested by the state constitution with control over other subjects or
activities plus some financial and institutional autonomy. Yet the division
of labor implicit in federal and federal-like arrangements is seldom complete and airtight. Some functions may, by constitutional mandate, be
shared between central and regional authorities. Frequently the central
government, by virtue of its control of the most productive tax sources, may
use it superior financial as well as political resources to operate in areas
nominally reserved to the provincial or regional governments. In other
cases, complementary functions may be vested in the central and the
regional governments—for example, interregional commerce, including
agricultural marketing in the central government and agricultural production in the regional authorities. Even for functions unambiguously assigned
to the center, such as interregional transportation, the complementary
control by the regional governments of land and land transactions produces
entanglements in program operations that involve development managers
at both levels. In some countries, municipal governments, especially those
of large urban centers, may be granted sufficient autonomy and control of
some subjects that officials of the central government must relate to their
municipal counterparts as equals. The financing and sharing of services in
such areas as health and construction must then be based on negotiation;
they cannot be effectively commanded.

Federal systems such as in India and Nigeria, or federal-like systems such
as in Malaysia and Mexico, compel development managers to take account
of organizations outside their own because resources they need are controlled by others or, alternatively, their services are needed by organizations
responsible to a level of government other than their own. These vertical
relationships have generated a branch of public administration known as

"intergovernmental relations"(Wright 1978). They may be regulated by general agreements arrived at by politicians, which nevertheless require continuous interpretation by managers as fresh problems arise, or they may be arrived at by ad hoc negotiation project by project, issue by issue. What facilitates compatible working arrangements is the understanding by both parties that they cannot accomplish their tasks without the cooperation of the other. Each party needs the other, each has an effective veto, each has strong incentives to cooperate.

In addition to expedient arrangements that enable them to carry on with the functions for which they are responsible, development managers must also represent the governmental authority to which they are responsible, promoting and protecting its particular interests. The resulting patterns of "cooperative federalism," involving shared costs, exchanges of services, and complementary responsibilities, tend to be even more complex and to require more bargaining than horizontal transactions among parallel bureaucracies under the same governmental authority. The standard situation in federal and federal-like structures requires the interaction of two organizations, each responsible to its own level of government. Not uncommon, however, are situations in which two or more agencies are involved from one or both levels of government. The number of actors may be multiplied when the agency of the central government must work with two or more provinces or states on matters that cross the latter's boundaries, an example being a water resources project on a stream or lake that flows between them. Federal arrangements are especially prone to produce interagency and interjurisdictional complexities that test the negotiating skills of development managers. Formal coordinating structures that governments sometimes improvise to regulate this complexity—for example, a regional development authority—are never organizationally self-sufficient. Some necessary services remain in the hands of agencies outside the regional authority. The participation of multiple agencies from two or more autonomous levels of government is still required, and so are the bargaining and negotiating by development managers that enable coordinated action.

When these conditions prevail, managers are not merely running their own organization, though that continues to be their main responsibility. They are compelled to adjust to the legal powers, the political influence, and the operating preferences of other organizations that are completely outside their control or even the control of the level of government to which they are responsible. Formal arrangements can be worked out to regulate these vertical relationships, or they can be handled by ad hoc and informal accommodations of a pragmatic kind that enable operations to proceed. At times, these conflicts may produce deadlocks that extend for considerable periods of time and have to be settled at the highest levels of government. Invariably they require negotiation and working arrangements among persons who are neither hierarchical superiors nor subordinates; whose goals, priorities, obligations, and expectations are not identical and, in fact, may conflict, and who owe organizational allegiance to a different set of political masters. Participating units may find it preferable to cooperate only on their own terms; impasses in such cumbersome machinery are averted and operations are lubricated by the informal problem-solving behavior of development managers.

SUPRASTATE ACTIVITIES

A note is appropriate here on suprastate projects or activities. Although there are painfully few instances of successful cooperation among two or more less developed countries (LDCs) in joint institutions or enterprises, a number of them do function, and they may become more common in the near future. These include development banks or financing institutions, research organizations, resource management units, and educational centers. The boards of directors of these organizations are usually composed of representatives of the participating states, while members of the the management staff may be seconded from the agencies of these governments. Suprastate entities may deal directly with individuals, enterprises, or communities in the participating countries, but more commonly they work with and through the established financial, educational, and research agencies of the member states.

Exchanges between the managers of the suprastate agencies and their professional counterparts in member governments define and continually adjust their mutual activities and working procedures. These are not dissimilar to those that evolve in federal states. Such relationships cannot be hierarchical; patterns of cooperation are achieved by negotiation among development managers in which the interests of the participating organizations at both levels are seldom neglected.

THE SPECIAL ROLE OF FOREIGN DONORS

For nearly four decades, the world of development managers has included agents of transnational development assistance organizations. They represent the foreign aid units of individual states (the bilateral donors) or of international organizations (the multilateral donors) or of nongovernmental, private-voluntary agencies. Foreign aid is a very pluralistic enterprise, involving literally scores of general-purpose or specialized actors. Their motives—political, strategic, commercial, humanitarian—are often mixed and not easily disentangled. The combined scale of these largely uncoordinated efforts is, however, very impressive. Recent data indicate that official development assistance from all sources, net of loan repayments, represents an annual flow of $56 billion to developing countries. Foreign aid annually finances 79,000 technicians, teachers, "experts," and advisors from industrialized societies working in developing countries and 126,000 students and other trainees from developing countries studying in the institutions of donor states (Chairman, Development Assistance Committee 1989). Although these magnitudes, especially on the financial side, are considered far below the real needs of developing countries or of norms established by international agreement, they are nonetheless considerable.

What is particularly relevant to this discussion is that a great many development activities in every sector of society, economy, and government involve the participation of development assistance agencies. A very small proportion of such assistance is awarded in cash with no strings attached. Accountable as they are to their governments or to their executive boards, foreign aid officials attempt to ensure that the resources they control are committed to activities that in their professional judgment will contribute positively to economic or social development and that the resources so committed are likely to be used with reasonable efficiency and probity and to reach their intended beneficiaries. The uses of these resources must be accounted for periodically by procedures and reports prescribed by and acceptable to the headquarters of the donor agencies.

Thus, at every stage of development assistance there is likely to be an active foreign presence. This occurs at the negotiation of agreements about the definition of the activity to be assisted, including the organizational structure or structures in which it will be housed and the inputs such as money, materials, equipment, personnel, and other resources that will be provided for the particular project by each party over the duration of the agreement. Initial agreements are normally revised or renegotiated on the basis of experience. At the implementation stage, the foreign agency may be present in the form of an individual or team of specialists or advisors who may be employees of the donor agency or of its contractors. They may be posted in the host country or they may fly in periodically for inspections and progress reviews.

Often the foreign personnel combine the roles of administrators, advisors, teachers, technical specialists, expediters of resources, and policemen, providing services, building institutions, and ensuring that resources contributed by the donor are used for their intended purposes. At the level of monitoring and evaluation, there is also a donor presence. At all stages of assisted activities, agents of a foreign government or of international or voluntary organizations participate in one or more of these roles, interfering in the operations of Third World governments in ways that the donor governments would never tolerate on their territory. This is true even when external assistance is financed by loans that must be serviced and eventually repaid with interest. Activities assisted by foreign aid cover the entire gamut of government operations from major construction to social and educational services, agricultural and industrial research, production and marketing, and all aspects of public administration and economic policy. On a small but increasing scale, foreign assistance is provided directly to private enterprises, voluntary associations, and local communities, supervised and monitored, however, by agents of the foreign donor. Legally and nominally, the donors are providing assistance to activities that continue to be managed by indigenous personnel, usually by officials of the host government. In practice, the donor agencies that provide the external resources are sometimes effectively in control.

The pervasive foreign presence in development operations represents the cross-cultural intersection and involvement of two or more bureaucracies in the same undertaking (Tendler 1975). Each of these bureaucracies is accountable to a different political authority, and each is subject to its own set of operating procedures and regulations, many with the force of law, that control the uses of funds, accounting and reporting routines, methods of procuring supplies and equipment, and technical standards. Often there are basic differences about how the organizations and activities should be managed. The resolution of these inherent differences has been labeled "development diplomacy," and the burden of this diplomacy falls mostly on development managers. The Third World managers must represent and protect the interests of their own governments and adhere to their laws, procedures, and policies while accommodating the requirements of donor agencies and moving ahead with the substantive project activities supported by donor assistance. Although the donor's requirements can often be circumvented or evaded—since the donor agency often wants the aid projects as much as does the host government—they are an important factor in the life of a development manager and cannot be disregarded.

To simplify these inherently complex arrangements, some donors insist that the activities they assist ("our projects") each be encapsulated in a special project unit that is exempt from the normal personnal and financial procedures of the host government and that the donor can closely supervise and effectively control. The main danger in these protected enclaves is the difficulty in transition to normal government operations once the donor leaves the scene. Most donor agencies have finally learned that prospects for "sustainability"—the capacity of the host government and society to carry on the activity once foreign assistance is withdrawn—are more favorable if donors work within the normal structures of the host government, in spite of the frustrations this may entail. The involvement of donors compels development managers to learn to accommodate the inconsistent and often conflicting requirements of two or more bureaucratic cultures.

Even with the best will in the world, the foreign presence imposes heavy burdens on the public administration of many developing countries; the weaker their administrative capabilities and the greater their dependence on foreign assistance, the heavier the burden. The burden of adjustment can affect every dimension of government from major policies to administrative procedures to program implementation. The incremental funds, the advanced technologies, the study and travel opportunities provided by foreign aid make this external presence more or less tolerable to government elites and senior program managers, but the tasks of day-to-day adjustment fall mainly on the latter. Many governments in LDCs provide a buffering mechanism, a high-level organization that handles formal arrangements with external donors and attempts to set up routines that reconcile the differing requirements of their government and of outsiders. Most of the problems occur, however, in the ongoing implementation of assisted programs; there the development manager is left to broker compromises—financial, procurement, personnel, reporting—that simultaneously satisfy the requirements and expectations of the government and of the donor agency and enable the project to move ahead. In effect, local managers share power with foreigners who control some of the resources needed to implement the program for which they are responsible. They may like and respect the guests, may welcome and appreciate the resources and other help they supply, but they also complicate life and constrain necessary freedom of action.

Thus development managers, trained and experienced in handling personnel or finance or in directing a service or regulatory activity within a standard bureaucratic framework, find themselves embroiled not only with other agencies of their own governments, but also with one or more representatives of a foreign government or international institution. The skills they must master to negotiate working arrangements with parallel bureaucracies in their own governments are of some help, but in coping with the foreigners they must be further stretched. The latter may require cross-cultural—diplomatic—sensitivities, often including the ability to function in a foreign language, to accommodate foreign guests, and to innovate and make do with unfamiliar substantive compromises and administrative expedients that are more or less acceptable both to their own superiors and to the donor agency.

MANAGING INCONGRUENCE

What I have outlined in this chapter are the manifestations and the consequences of incongruence among two or more official bureaucratic organizations that become entangled in the same activity. Each such organization has its distinctive mission and legal foundations, its own professional orientation, program priorities, methods of operation, resources for which it is accountable, criteria of accountability, and links with the public—in effect, its distinctive bureaucratic culture. They normally prefer to maintain exclusive control over activities within their substantive areas of responsibility, since this protects the integrity of their procedures and minimizes uncertainty. Thus they guard their boundaries; maintain verticle patterns of communication, authority, and accountability; and resist coordination or shared responsibility with other entities. When, however, they are confronted with the necessity of participating in an activity jointly with another organization that has a different orientation, priorities, and procedures, some adjustments become unavoidable. The degree of adjustment may reflect differential bureaucratic power, the stronger partner dominating the transaction; or it may reflect the practical problems of accommodating the personnel, material resources, and schedules of two or more organizations that are governed by different rules, priorities, and procedures and are accustomed to operating independently. Though politicians and interest groups are sometimes involved, the negotiations are normally handled, the deals are struck and then implemented, by development managers from the participating organizations.

The unit of interagency coordination is either an ongoing activity or a specific time-bound project. The need for coordination produces both structural and procedural expedients. The most common structures are committees in which representatives of the participating agencies work out policies and patterns for interorganizational cooperation. These can occur at the highest levels of government, in cabinet or interministerial committees. There may be high-level structures to coordinate foreign aid, in which representatives of donor agencies as well as officials of the host government participate. In the field, there may be a variety of structures, among them authorities for administering large-scale regional development schemes, whose membership consists of the various departments and parastatals that contribute resources to the project. At the district level, there may be one or more working groups chaired by a senior official to integrate and expedite the efforts of two or more departments contributing to a set of related activities. There may be project committees similarly constituted to facilitate the performance of all the agencies involved in a particular development project.

What these various structures have in common is the principle and practice of representation. Separate organizational identities and interests remain intact, but their participation in specific common enterprises must be coordinated. Coordination can be accomplished by "strong" or "weak" structures. In strong structures, the coordinator actually controls funds and is responsible for operations; other agencies providing inputs for the project have an incentive to cooperate on terms set by the project director. In weak structures, which are much more common, the coordinating authority or facilitator must rely primarily on bureaucratic status, access to higher- level officials, and especially political skills to induce or cajole the cooperation of other agencies on terms acceptable to both parties. Although the various agencies seldom refuse to cooperate, they can drag their feet and participate at their own convenience, preferring to focus their energies and assign priority to the functional programs for which they are directly responsible. Thus a tax bureau, under pressure to increase collections in support of a structural adjustment program to reduce the fiscal deficit, may have to cope with a public prosecutor's office that prefers to allocate its limited resources to narcotics offenses or other forms of criminal behavior.

Normal budgetary practice in most governments allocates funds to functional ministries and their operating bureaus, which design and manage their own programs. Interagency coordination is usually accomplished by weak structures or by informal arrangements. On the other hand, capital budgeting and foreign aid are usually project focused; funding and implementing powers are committed to a single project authority that results in relatively strong coordinating structures. Time-bound projects supported by capital budgets or by foreign aid usually benefit from more effective coordination than ongoing activities financed by operating budgets. For example, interagency cooperation is easier to achieve for constructing irrigation works than for their subsequent operation and maintenance or for the ongoing farming activities that utilize water from the irrigation system. The transition from construction financed by foreign aid to operating budget support often leads to strains and even breakdowns in interagency coordination.

There are two main methods or processes of interagency coordination, the formal and the nonformal. Formal agreements are contracts that specify the modes of participation by the contracting organizations and what their respective inputs and responsibilities should be. These can apply to continuing operations or to specific time-bound projects. Most foreign assistance projects are precisely regulated by formal agreements between the host government and the donor organization. But while such formal agreements outline the goals and specify the contributions of the two parties, implementation invariably raises numerous issues that must be settled by ad hoc negotiation on the part of development managers.

Formal coordinating structures are vulnerable to rigidity and deadlock as the participating parties jockey to promote and defend their own organizational interests (Chaturvedi 1988). When meetings become routine, participation declines because the outcomes no longer justify the effort. Much more effective are ad hoc working parties focused on concrete projects or sets of tasks that clearly require joint efforts. When the tasks have been accomplished, the ad hoc structures lapse. For some ongoing or seasonal activities, coordination may have to be sustained or renewed periodically. The operative principle is that the more concrete the tasks and the less formal the machinery, the more likely that coordination will succeed. Formal structures tend to inhibit rather than facilitate cooperation across bureaucratic lines.

Thus, the most common, most effective method of interagency coordination is the nonformal pattern of general understandings and expedient accommodation dictated by practical necessity. This is the pattern that would be recommended for the aforementioned tax bureau seeking more accommodative performance from the prosecutor's office. Neither party has unreasonable expectations or makes unacceptable demands on the other, and they cooperate without the benefit or hindrance of a formal structure, weak or strong. Negotiations may be stressful and frustrating, especially to the weaker agency in any particular transaction. All parties are careful to protect the interests of their parent organization and to conform to its policies, priorities, and rules. Within these constraints, they find the space to contribute their skills and resources to another activity where the need is evident on terms that are bargained out; reciprocity, where needed, is expected. The terms of these nonformal arrangements are routinely negotiated and then implemented by development managers, who learn by experience that the real scope of their responsibilities cannot be contained within a single organization and that the management of interorganizational incongruity is part of their job that calls for political as well as administrative skills.

HORIZONTAL RESPONSIBILITIES
AND THE MANAGERIAL ROLE

The responsibilities of public development managers cannot be limited to their traditional vertical dimension in a single bureaucratic organization, accountable exclusively to hierarchical superiors, directing subordinates similarly responsible to them. Increasingly, government-sponsored activities cannot be confined within the tight boundaries of a single organization. The horizontal or interorganizational dimension of the managerial role arises because of the impossibility of drawing organizational boundaries that coincide exactly with the policies or concrete activities to which governments are committed. Despite efforts to achieve self-sufficiency and total control over the resources they need, bureaucratic agencies find it necessary or are required to share responsibility for some activities, to draw on resources and skills controlled by other organizations, or to respond to external requests for assistance. All activities involving foreign aid require similar horizontal communication and coordination. Special coordinating structures may be created to house complex activities, but these tend to be endowed with few resources and limited powers; they too are compelled to induce the cooperation of other organizations. Although some patterns of interagency exchanges and coordination may be prescribed by law and others arranged at the political level, most such undertakings are designed, implemented, and adjusted by development managers.

Horizontal relationships introduce elements of complexity into the lives of managers. They may generate moral dilemmas as managers must weigh primary allegiance to their own organizations into which they have been socialized and on which their career advancement is likely to depend, against the manifest need for their assistance on the part of parallel organizations and programs. Attempts to reconcile these competing pressures and obligations confront managers with ethical challenges that will be elaborated in Chapter 7. Such moral sensitivities and political skills are required to a much lesser degree for conventional managerial roles in a single organization. When hierarchical authority does not apply, working relationships must depend on the diplomatic skills of bargaining and negotiating with counterparts who cannot be commanded, who control resources of their own, and whose operating priorities are not congruent with those of their prospective partners. As previously indicated, informal friendships derived from family, ethnic, old-school tie, common work experience, or leisure activities and attention to cultivating such relationships can prove to be critical lubricants to interagency cooperation among development managers.

The talents required to manage such relationships are not equally distributed among all managers, but they can be fostered and rewarded. Management education should sensitize students and trainees to this dimension of their professional responsibilities and cultivate the requisite political skills. The most effective method for such training is through case study analysis, which compels students to share vicariously the agony of conflicting pressures and the implications of alternative choices that confront managers in these situations. In the division of leadership roles, some managers may be assigned to concentrate on internal tasks, others on external relations, though as they advance into higher ranks, political skills assume greater importance. Among the techniques that can help managers master the complexity that they encounter is the ability to map their working environments (White 1990). Astute managers do this instinctively, but this is a set of methods that can be taught and cultivated. By identifying the organizations and political-interest groups that are likely to impinge on managers' activities, by estimating their resources, their needs, their real and potential influence, and even their strategies, managers can bring some order into their external environments. Instead of passively coping or muddling through, they can attempt to anticipate the demands that are likely to be made on their resources and the likely responses of others to their requests for assistance. Development managers can prepare their tactics, be ready with alternatives, and thereby limit surprises in their political environments.

Reward systems should take account not only of the vertical, but also of the horizontal dimensions of managerial performance, of effectiveness in handling external relationships, of securing needed assistance on favorable terms, and of accommodating the reasonable demands of counterpart government agencies.

The emphasis on interagency or horizontal relationships cannot merely be tacked on to conventional management education curricula or performance-appraisal instruments. It is not enough to incorporate them under the commodious but vague rubric of "public relations." This is a dimension of the management role that is essential to policy and program implementation (White 1990; Mazmanian and Sabatier 1983). It merits explicit attention not only in management education, as I have indicated, but also in job descriptions and performance evaluations, where specific sections should be reserved for this element of the managerial role. Bureaucratic hierarchies normally emphasize vertical responsibilities and tend to relegate horizontal relationships to minor or incidental importance in job peformance. To compensate for this bias, incentives should be built into the reward systems of organizations so that performance along the interorganizational dimensions of management becomes a determining factor in a manager's career advancement.

Though most bureaucratic careers will continue to be dominated by vertically specialized organizations, provision should routinely be made for complementary organizations and coordinating officials to provide testimony evaluating the effectiveness of managers in their interagency performance. Personnel actions involving senior managers should be reviewed by boards that include individuals outside their own agency so that their interorganizational performance can be stipulated as a major criterion and accorded substantial weight in promotions and other rewards. The incentive effects of such arrangements can be considerable. Because interorganizational coordination is so important to policy implementation and to program performance, development managers should expect that this dimension of their responsibilities will be a significant factor affecting their career advancement.

Interorganizational coordination cannot be limited, however, to agencies of government. The management of pluralistic development strategies must incorporate the energies and the interests of nongovernmental parties as well.

5

ALTERNATIVE CHANNELS FOR SERVICE PROVISION

STATE MONOPOLY OR PRAGMATIC PLURALISM

THERE IS NO A PRIORI REASON FOR STATE MONOPOLY OF THE SERVICES ESSENTIAL to society except for those related to national defense and law enforcement. This is contrary to the statist position that, in its many versions, has exerted a powerful influence on political thought and practice during the twentieth century. The statist argument holds that only the state is qualified to represent the general will or the common interests of society, since any lesser grouping necessarily reflects a particular, limited, parochial, and self-regarding set of interests. The state, on the other hand, is the most reliable agent and trustee for society in defining and pursuing such cherished collective goals as national unity, economic modernization, and social justice. Therefore, as the statist argument goes, governments should sponsor and, when necessary, undertake any activities that are essential to society as a whole, including any that are critical to social and economic development. The monistic and centralized view of the state commanded widespread support in the post–World War II years, which witnessed the emergence of independent polities in most less developed countries (LDCs). It helped to justify the tendencies of the elites of the new states to act as economic planners, entrepreneurs, and managers and in many cases to incorporate a vast array of economic activities into the apparatus of government.

The historical record has demonstrated convincingly that most governments, including Third World states, tend to be poor economic entrepreneurs and even worse managers of economic enterprises. Although the reasons are complex, and there are many specific exceptions, the weight of evidence indicates that government operation, while displacing initiatives and managerial capabilities elsewhere in society, fails to provide the incentives needed for the determined and sustained pursuit of economic efficiency.

Owner cultivation has proved to be far more productive per unit of land and of labor than state farms. In manufacturing, marketing, finance, and trade, profit-seeking entrepreneurs subject to competitive market incentives and discipline are more likely to be innovative, use their resources efficiently, and respond to consumer demand. So convincing is the recent record in Eastern Europe and the Third World that a consensus has emerged: When economic dynamism and efficiency are the goals, the presumption should favor private entrepreneurship, ownership, and management of agriculture, industry, and commerce, regulated mainly by competitive market processes.

This does not imply, however, that the state should, or indeed is destined to, wither away. It is state monopoly, not the institutional state, that is likely to wither—an important distinction. In addition to its monopoly on national defense, internal security, and law enforcement, only the state can operate a legal system that defines and protects the personal and property rights of individuals and corporate enterprises. It must establish, enforce, and adjust the macroeconomic policies that set the parameters for economic activity. It must manage external political, economic, and cultural relations. It must, in the interest of public health, safety, and convenience, regulate such economic and social activities as land use, labor standards, and consumer safety. It must protect the physical environment from dangerous pollutants, abusive exploitation, and degradation. It must finance, operate, and maintain such vital collective goods as the physical infrastructure of roads, harbors, airports, electric power, water supply, and sites and services for urban housing. It must provide the social infrastructure of education, public health, and environmental sanitation as well as the scientific and technological research required to enhance productivity in agriculture and industry. These are minimal requirements for all governments. As economic growth permits, governments are drawn into networks of welfare services, since governments are better equipped than markets to promote the values of social security and equitable access to basic services and to protect the weaker and more vulnerable elements of society against the harsher outcomes of competitive market forces. It comes as no surprise that in the most successful private-enterprise and market-based economies—the members of the Organization for Economic Cooperation and Development (OECD)—government at all levels takes an average of thirty-five percent of gross national product (GNP) for the provision of public services.

What this brief discussion implies is that the state in LDCs need not and should not aspire to operate the productive sectors of the economy or to monopolize economic and social services.[1] The state should, instead, attempt to promote and stimulate economic initiatives and management capabilities in society wherever they can be found, to arrive at expedient divisions of labor between the agencies of the state and nongovernmental actors, and to shape cooperative patterns among them, each doing what it is best equipped to do. The formula is one of pragmatic pluralism in which the state establishes and enforces the rules, but at the level of operations it performs as one of many actors participating in the production and provision of economic and social goods and services. In this chapter, I identify and explore the major institutional actors with which governments must work out compatible divisions of labor for managing development activities. In the next chapter, I indicate how these divisions of labor can be converted into viable service networks.

PRIVATE ENTERPRISE

The collapse of the once vaunted Soviet centrally planned, bureaucratically managed, and state-owned economy combined with the economic crises afflicting so many state-dominated LDCs have confirmed the long-standing creed of capitalist economics: that privately owned and managed profit-seeking enterprises operating in competitive markets are more likely than state enterprises to achieve efficiency in resource use as well as responsiveness to consumers. The simple explanation is that competitive market incentives and discipline are conducive to these results. This does not mean that state-owned enterprises cannot operate efficiently, as many do. Nor does it mean that market economies always produce efficiency. In Third World settings, markets may function ineffectively in the absence of physical infrastructure, financial institutions, and competitive enterprise. Private firms are prone to use their economic muscle or their political influence to seek economic rents: to limit competition; achieve a monopoly position; or demand protection, subsidies, and similar political favors that vitiate the incentive effects of market competition. The institution of profit-seeking private enterprise is not, ipso facto, virtuous, socially responsible, or trouble free.

Nevertheless the weight of historical evidence is compelling enough to produce the following policy implications: When there is a choice, governments should promote and facilitate the development of market institutions and of vigorous private enterprise in the main productive sectors, especially in farming, manufacturing, construction, finance, and commerce. The emphasis should not be on a handful of large firms controlled, as they often are, by foreign interests or by politically connected operatives that depend on government patronage, but on numerous medium and small businesses willing to take their chances in competitive markets.

Some political elites continue to challenge this policy because they distrust, suspect, and are morally offended by the acquisitive, self-seeking motives and behavior of private businesspeople, whether indigenous or foreign, preferring the values of social solidarity over individualistic profit seeking. Some object to sharing power with the private sector, a suspicion that is aggravated by envy of the (ill-gotten) wealth achieved by successful businesspeople, especially if they are foreigners or members of unpopular ethnic minorities. Others seek ways to exploit the private sector in return for subsidies or preferential treatment, an informal tax on private enterprise in exchange for privileges that compromise economic efficiency. These are real possibilities and they must be dealt with, but none of them are sufficient to override the basic strategy of relying primarily on private enterprise and market discipline for economic growth and efficiency.

This strategy imposes on development managers in government a multitude of responsibilities to which I have already alluded but that require further elaboration. The first is the maintenance of a policy environment that provides consistent incentives and rewards for enterprise, that makes it easy for businesses to be started, protects their property and contracts, encourages their expansion, and enables them to enjoy the fruits of their success. This implies a simple and nondiscriminatory tax regime that produces needed revenues while encouraging the reinvestment of profits. It implies a cautious policy on protection and on subsidies, which businesspeople, including farmers, are certain to demand. Although protection and subsidies are sometimes useful for reducing risks and stimulating innovation, once granted they cannot easily be withdrawn. They become crutches for inefficient firms, a tax on the economy for the benefit of privileged minorities, stifling market incentives. Some Third World economies have become strangled in networks of official subsidies to producers and consumers, often with contradictory effects, such as tariff protection for fertilizer manufacturers combined with price subsidies to encourage fertilizer use by small farmers, some of whom immediately sell the unneeded product at a profit to larger producers. Development managers are well-advised to resist demands for subsidies as a means to stimulate desired economic behavior, despite the political pressures that usually accompany such demands.

There are many government activities that facilitate private enterprise. One of the most essential is the establishment and maintenance of physical infrastructure: highways, bridges, ports, electric power, and telephone service. These are costly to build and maintain, but provide essential external economies for business operations. The demand for such investments is imperative and inexhaustible, while the financial and managerial burdens on government are enormous. One consequence of pressures to expand such facilities is that governments systematically tend to neglect and underfinance the maintenance of these costly installations, despite the high price this soon exacts in nonfunctioning equipment and eroded facilities that must eventually be replaced or rebuilt. The proper maintenance of structures and equipment in the public sector is a responsibility for which officialdom in most LDCs and international donors as well have not made adequate financial provision or committed sufficient managerial resources.

Parallel to the physical infrastructure, is the government-provided social infrastructure for the economy, especially its educational system. The education that is needed is not confined to formal schooling, but should provide opportunities for nonformal learning in many activities from agricultural extension to health practices. Public education, for which there is also an inexhaustible demand, provides the private sector with a literate and numerate labor force and with high-level technical, scientific, professional, and similar workers. The continual upgrading of its human resources is regarded by many as the most valuable contribution government can make to social and economic development (Verspoor 1988).

Though private and voluntary initiatives may also be present, government is the main provider of management training at all levels, from professional education to basic management skills and procedures for local government and small-enterprise development (Kerrigan and Luke 1987). The political challenge in the education sector is how to reconcile with limited means the intense demand for general education at all levels with the compelling and relatively costly needs of government and industry for specialized education in a variety of disciplines and professions, including management.

Parallel to education is the research function, the innovation and extension of practices that increase efficiency and help solve the problems of production and marketing, especially in agriculture and industry (Pinstrup-Andersen 1982). For the most part, applied research in these areas is the responsibility of government, though foreign donors are often willing to provide substantial assistance in developing research capacities. One of the main challenges in research management is to ensure that the problems addressed by scientific staffs are those that respond to the practical needs of farmers and businesspeople so that results can be directly useful to them. This calls for a style of research management in which the prospective users of research findings are represented in the selection and definition of research topics and have the opportunity to participate in their factories, workshops, and fields in the implementation of research projects and in the testing and refinement of results (Whyte and Boynton 1983).

In these ways, a strategy of economic development that relies primarily on private operations and market processes is facilitated and supported by a complex of indispensable activities that continue to impose heavy financial and managerial burdens on government. This strategy does not award carte blanche to the private sector to abuse its workers (including women and children), victimize consumers, pollute the environment, indulge in monopolistic practices, misuse the funds of depositors, evade taxes, construct unsafe buildings in urban areas, and so on. Governments must regulate such antisocial practices, establishing rules and procedures that may be regarded as politically adversarial and economically burdensome by those against whom they are directed. Those who must manage regulatory programs are likely to be importuned by regulated parties for exceptions and sympathetic treatment, often accompanied by offers of bribes or threats of political reprisal. Development managers must walk the fine line between their regulatory responsibilities and the legitimate convenience of the subjects of their regulation. The implementation of regulatory measures can be negotiated with regulated parties through their interest associations to minimize onerous paperwork and reporting requirements and prevent harassment that is not essential to enforcement. Although politicians tend to be drawn into major regulatory decisions, their interpretation and application, which have important substantive as well as procedural implications, are usually the responsibility of development managers.

Pressures for privatization and marketization are often accompanied by demands for deregulation: to control the behavior of economic actors by substituting automatic and allegedly self-correcting competitive market discipline—the invisible hand—for more visible administrative measures. Another version of this approach is to foster self-regulation by business groups, expressing considerable confidence in the public-spirited motivation of profit-seeking enterprises. Aside from freeing businesses of needless and often costly restraints on their initiative and freedom of action, one purpose of deregulation is to limit opportunities for officials to extract bribes from businesses, large and small, and thereby to minimize the scope and incidence of official corruption. Governments must foster and facilitate the dynamism of private enterprise while protecting society against the abuses of unrestrained greed. In some Third World countries, overregulation has hampered economic development, inflated government payrolls, and encouraged official corruption; in others, the public has been insufficiently protected. Some regulations may be obsolete, unenforced, or easily evaded, reducing respect for government. Senior development managers have the responsibility to subject the regulatory regime that they are enforcing to periodic reassessment to determine whether it is accomplishing its intended objectives, whether these objectives contribute to economic and social development, and whether the procedures meet the tests of efficiency and public convenience.

Privatization, marketization, and deregulation reduce but cannot eliminate the governmental or "publicness" dimension of business operations (Bozeman 1987). Private enterprise must function within macroeconomic parameters set by government, comply with or attempt to evade taxes and regulations imposed by government, and capitalize on opportunities provided by government agencies, military and civilian, as customers and

patrons. Private enterprises are not merely targets of government initiatives; they also attempt to influence the behavior of government by a variety
of methods ranging from interest-group lobbying to bribery and similar
techniques of persuasion. In the many interfaces between government and
privately owned businesses, even in economies that respect market processes, development managers are important participants in the shaping and
implementation of policies and in the negotiation of individual arrangements.

CONTRACTING TO PRIVATE ENTERPRISE

An expression of the movement toward privatization is the process of
contracting for private operation of activities sponsored and financed by the
state. Instead of undertaking activities directly, governments arrange by
competitive contracting for their performance by private firms, capitalizing
on their presumed more efficient management capabilities, technical skills,
operating flexibility, and freedom from political interference. The anticipated result is more effective, lower-cost performance because of the profit
incentives that drive private firms, which are able to avoid both the
cumbersome civil service methods and the abuses of patronage associated
with government operations.

Contracting with private firms and even voluntary agencies has proved
to be a feasible method of limiting the scale of government operations for
activities that must nevertheless remain government responsibilities. A
precondition for contracting, however, is the availability of firms competent
to perform and willing to work for government. The availability of money
stimulates the entrepreneurial spirit, often resulting in fly-by-night competitors for government business. Some firms that come into being to win
government contracts may emerge as substantial businesses able to survive
and prosper in competitive markets. In this way, the contract mechanism
may strengthen the authentic private sector. Those contractors, however,
that remain dependent on government business have a greater incentive to
cultivate the favor of politicians and senior administrators than to deliver
efficient services.

The contracting method, in functions as varied as construction, facilities
maintenance, waste disposal, military procurement, hospital services, and
even prison operations, may limit the operations of the state and provide
more cost-effective goods and services (Roth 1987). But the method is not
trouble free. The scandals in U.S. military procurement and chronic abuses
in highway contracting suggest the problems that this system can pose for
Third World states. The contracting process must be kept competitive and
free of collusion, otherwise monopoly contractors can rip off the government financially while providing the public with substandard services.

Standards of performance and costs must be meticulously specified in the contracting instruments, performance must be systematically monitored, and penalties must be assessed for deficient results. The methods employed for monitoring are mainly periodic reports supplemented by inspections, product testing, financial and performance auditing, and the encouragement of reactions from consumers.

Contracting has the effect of transferring substantial routine functions of government to the operation of private firms or nonprofit voluntary agencies. It leaves government as financier with an array of supervisory responsibilities, among them specifying detailed scopes of work, inviting and assessing competitive bids, negotiating agreements, monitoring performance, and enforcing the terms and conditions of contracts. Many such disputes can end up in court. In the absence of supervision, which can be a significant managerial cost, governments quickly lose control of contractors who are prone to cut corners in order to enhance profits. It is an article of faith among partisans of free enterprise that private-sector operations, including contracting, are inherently more efficient and less corrupt than those managed directly by government. The available data are more ambiguous, since collusion, corruption, inefficiency, and insensitivity to the public find their way into contracting arrangements also.

In LDCs, contracting can facilitate the emergence of viable private firms and thus promote economic development, as long as a competitive environment can be assured. Although it can relieve government of the burden of direct operation, especially of routine functions, and ensure more cost-effective performance of activities that continue to be financed by the state, government remains responsible for both the expenditures and the results. The enforcement of these responsibilities, the protection of the public interest in the use of these resources and in the results, and the negotiation, supervision, and monitoring of contract operations represent substantial ongoing costs to government (Moore 1989). The burden of supervision and enforcement falls to public-sector managers who must cultivate a set of skills that are distinctive to contract operations. They are likely to be compensated for their efforts much less generously than the private-sector counterparts they supervise.

PUBLIC-SECTOR ENTERPRISE: THE HYBRID

This is a dimension of political economy and of public administration that has, until recently, been neglected by both economists and students of management. Yet in many LDCs a large share of the economy, especially of its modern sectors, is owned, financed, and operated by government. This includes not only the "lumpy" investments in natural monopolies such as electric power, telephone and telegraph, railways and ports, but also large enterprises in natural resource development, especially petroleum and other minerals; manufacturing industries; airlines; agricultural marketing; banking and finance; and, in some countries, hotels, newspapers, and retail establishments. Some enterprises in the public sector were inherited from the colonial past. Others resulted from the apparent disinterest or inability of local investors to venture into activities deemed necessary by government or from the determination of political elites to limit foreign participation in such activities or deny their control to domestic ethnic minorities.

Some failing businesses were rescued from bankruptcy and taken over by the state to maintain services considered to be essential or to avoid additional unemployment. Others were started or nationalized for ideological reasons, to keep government in control of the "commanding heights" of the economy, since the decision criteria for these basic enterprises would have to be the long-term needs of the national economy rather than the short-term profits of private owners. Such leaders as Nasser, Nehru, Nkrumah, and Nyerere, Third World exponents of Fabian socialism, had little confidence in or respect for market processes or for the morality of profit-seeking private enterprise. However diverse their origins, most governments in LDCs had, by the 1980s, gathered under their direct control and operational management significant portions of their national economy. In the sixteen countries of Francophone Africa, for example, the two thousand or more public enterprises account for an average of more than sixteen percent of gross domestic product (GDP) and twenty-four percent of fixed investment (Saulniers 1990).

These parastatal enterprises are owned, financed, and managed by governments, though specific patterns have varied. Some operate as government corporations, some under standard company laws, but in most cases they are formally responsible to a government ministry that exercises a determining voice in their investment programs, pricing policies, labor relations, and choice of product lines. Because they normally produce goods or services intended to be sold on national and sometimes international markets, the principle is generally accepted that they need greater managerial flexibility than normal government operations—the conventional assumption being that government operations are inherently and necessarily cumbersome—and freedom from political interference. Consequently, they have been for the most part exempted from civil service rules and allowed to employ and compensate staff and manage employee relations according to market practices. They are usually relieved of the detailed expenditure controls normally enforced by finance ministries and government auditors, though they are often required to take their turn in line for scarce foreign exchange.

This managerial flexibility has been frequently violated, however, by the prominent role of senior civil servants on management boards, by their tendency to draw management personnel from the ranks of the civil service, and by the tendency of governments to control their investment decisions, limit their discretion in setting and adjusting prices, and enforce comparability in compensation between government officials and the staffs of parastatal enterprises. Public corporations often become dumping grounds for needy relatives and political supporters, retired military officers and civil servants, unemployed school leavers, and other underqualified and redundant personnel.

The intention has been that these enterprises be governed by market criteria, earning enough net revenue to cover operating costs and to produce surpluses (profits) for modernization and expansion or dividends to the government that holds their shares. Though there have been notable exceptions, the dismal performance of public enterprises in most Third World countries has betrayed these expectations. Many have become chronic money losers, surviving on public subsidies that have exacerbated financial pressures on government, while providing inferior and often unreliable products to the public. The main reason for these failures has been the absence of incentives and often of opportunities for management to innovate and to operate as efficient market-oriented enterprises. The aforementioned government interventions on investments, prices, personnel, labor relations, and product lines have demoralized their management and condemned many government enterprises to certain economic failure.

Though the United Nations set up a small unit early in the 1970s to assist member countries, with few exceptions the phenomenon was neglected by academics and donor agencies (Hanson 1959; Ramanadham 1984). Schools of public administration tended to regard public enterprise as too "economic" for their professional skills, while schools of business, concentrating on the private sector, insisted on regarding the management of parastatals as no different from the management of private firms. This situation changed dramatically beginning in the early 1980s because of the economic recession that threatened financial viability and produced debt crises in so many Third World countries, combined with the simultaneous reascendancy of neoclassical economics as the official policy of the British and especially the U.S. governments. The problems of public-sector enterprise have surfaced as a major concern of donor agencies, especially the World Bank, prompting a reassessment of the role of parastatals in economic development (Jones and Moran 1982; Heath 1990).

The solution preferred by the donor community is divestment and privatization when feasible, closing failing enterprises or selling them off to the private sector. A few governments have been persuaded to move aggressively in this direction and some more hesitantly; as a result, few new public enterprises have been created since the early 1980s. Venture capital is, however, not abundant in LDCs and there continue to be attractive and relatively safe investment opportunities for private entrepreneurs in land and urban real estate. There is little incentive for private buyers to risk taking over money-losing businesses, while governments are reluctant to sell profitable firms at a discount. Capital markets are thin, and the large investments needed to take control of natural regulated monopolies such as electric power are seldom available. Many governments remain ambivalent about foreign investment or the participation of ethnic minorities, especially in certain key sectors of their economies such as natural resources. As a consequence of this combination of factors, the expansion of public enterprise in LDCs has ceased, some divestment and privatization have occurred, and the government sector is likely to constitute a diminishing share of LDCs' economies in the future. But most existing state enterprises will continue to operate under government control.

The challenge today is to reorient public enterprises so that they can make positive contributions to the economic development of their countries. For the regulated monopolies, for example, the generation and distribution of electricity, this means that they should function at levels of efficiency and provide standards of service comparable to current international norms for such industries. Others must be able to perform profitably under competitive market conditions. Governments are being urged to relax and even abandon many of the controls they have imposed on these enterprises and allow their managers the freedom to manage, constrained only by the laws and regulations that apply to all businesses, and hold the managers strictly accountable for results. Governments' main instrument of control, borrowed from successful French experience, seems likely to be the annual performance contract negotiated between government and enterprise management (Nellis 1988; Bennett 1990). These contracts stipulate the financial, production, and service goals that managers are expected to achieve and the resources that will be available to them. Managers are then allowed full discretion, free of political and ministerial interference in their daily operations, to produce and market their output and to maintain an economically efficient and viable enterprise. Their performance is subject to rigorous annual audit and review to assess compliance with their contracts. Bonuses are available for outstanding performance, while deficient results can precipitate management changes. The notorious, costly, and criminal abuses committed by public-enterprise managers in such firms as Pertamina in Indonesia and Pemex in Mexico demonstrate, however, that enterprise managers must be subjected to public vigilance and controls as well as provided with performance incentives such as those visualized by the contract arrangements.

The efficacy of the contract arrangement in LDCs has not been conclusively demonstrated. Its underlying premise is that public enterprise can be depoliticized, that politicians and senior officials will be willing to limit themselves to supervisory, monitoring, and controlling roles similar to corporate boards of directors in large private firms. It also means that competent enterprise managers are available. These hybrid managers must know enough about how government works to be able to negotiate effectively with the ministry that supervises them, with the treasury, and with the central bank. They must be able to cope with the entreaties, pressures, and threats of politicians, interest groups, and labor unions. They must also know how to operate an industrial or financial enterprise profitably under market conditions. Whether the education, research, and consulting services needed to cultivate and support this pattern of management are best situated in business schools or schools of public administration or in institutions specializing in this function is not yet clear. But the need to provide for the basic training and continual upgrading and updating of the skills of this critical and specialized cadre of public development managers is beyond dispute. To the incentives provided by the new contract arrangements must be added the managerial skills needed to operate economically viable public-sector enterprises under Third World conditions.

VOLUNTARY (NONGOVERNMENTAL) ASSOCIATIONS

Organized capacity to provide the goods and services required for social and economic development is not confined to government or to profit-seeking private enterprise. Private profit is not the only incentive that stimulates purposeful, efficient, and sustained collective action. The inclination to associate and to pursue common objectives by voluntary action, independently of government and without the expectation of economic profit, is a universal phenomenon. The result is a heterogeneous set of associations organized in a variety of ways, committed to a variety of goals, and performing a variety of tasks. Some are initiated by upper-class individuals as advocacy groups that also provide services in pursuit of their social mission, an example being family-planning agencies. Some originate in charitable impulses, often under religious auspices; over time they may build and operate schools, orphanages, hospitals, and old-age homes; in recent years, they have expanded from welfare to community improvement and other forms of small-scale economic development activities. Some of these activities may be assisted by foreign religious groups, secular bodies, and even international government donors. The management of their operations is, however, based on the nonprofit principle and they are independent, sometimes fiercely independent, of government.

Many grassroots voluntary associations represent responses to collective needs experienced at the local level—to clean, maintain, and repair religious structures or school buildings; provide for the upkeep of access roads; operate small irrigation systems or cattle dips; or provide readily available local sources of credit. Many of these organizations are informal, operate according to familiar local practices and management methods, are reinforced by kinship ties, are accountable only to their members, and escape the attention of governments. Some such associations, however, are complex in their functions, sophisticated in their management practices, and formal. For example, agricultural cooperatives that purchase, store, and even manufacture production inputs, furnish credit and life insurance for their members, operate processing and transportation facilities, and provide marketing services may be substantial enterprises regulated and assisted by government. They may require legal charters and be governed according to bylaws that stipulate the responsibilities of their officers and prescribe rigorous bookkeeping arrangements. Voluntary associations may be federated into regional and even national structures that expand the services available to their members and enable them to function as pressure groups in the political arena. The scale and efficiency on which a voluntary organization can operate is illustrated by the Grameen Bank in Bangladesh, which makes production loans to groups of landless male and female workers; through five hundred branches that serve three million borrowers, it has achieved a loan repayment rate of ninety-nine percent.

Some associations are brought into being and assisted by government agencies to facilitate the management and maintenance of services for which governments are responsible, such as health centers, irrigation systems, community forests, or neighborhood sanitation. Most of them, however, are the result of local initiative by individuals or groups responding to grassroots needs and opportunities for collective action independently of government (Esman and Uphoff 1984).

What characterizes voluntary associations apart from the variety of functions they perform, their autonomy and self-management, and accountability to their membership is their impressive capacity for action (Carroll and Montgomery 1987; Chambers 1983; Wanasinghe 1979). Voluntary associations have demonstrated the ability to mobilize substantial resources in the form of labor, money, information, and specialized skills, including management. They can convert these resources into goods and services that benefit their individual members and their communities. They are often prepared to assume collective economic risks, for example, by investing in transport or processing equipment, that would be impossible for their individual members. They can and do operate and manage production, processing, marketing, and financial facilities and installations.

They can provide reliable and accurate information about the specific circumstances, needs, preferences, and conveniences of their members, which enables government agencies, often remote from knowledge of local conditions and experience, to adapt their activities more effectively to local realities and requirements. Through their own organizational channels, they can retail to their members information, goods, and services that governments can provide only to whole communities but not to individual households. And capitalizing on the strength of their numbers, local organizations can empower the weaker sectors of society to make convincing claims on government and on official bureaucracies for the services to which they are entitled, to resist and counteract corrupt and exploitative practices by locally posted civil servants, and to compel a greater measure of responsiveness and accountability by officialdom to local publics.

What should be the relationships between voluntary organizations and governments? Some proponents of voluntary action advocate complete autonomy for voluntary associations, the maintenance of arm's-length relationships with government. They are so hostile toward and suspicious of what they believe to be the inherent abusiveness, corruption, and incompetence of officialdom that, they argue, only by complete and principled independence from government can voluntary organizations hope to reflect and serve the interests of their members (Rahman 1984). Contact with government is inherently corrupting; it conduces inevitably to dependency and domination, which are likely to prove fatal to authentic people's organizations. Such militant independence can, however, condemn voluntary associations to very narrow ranges of activities. Government agencies are not necessarily, uniformly, or irremediably corrupt and incompetent. They usually possess technical skills, specialized information, physical resources, and funds that are needed by voluntary organizations to expand and enrich the services they provide for their members. Voluntary associations can enhance their own collective capabilities by tapping resources that only governments are in a position to provide; government agencies, in turn, can increase their effectiveness by linking their operations to the grassroot networks and facilities controlled by the voluntary organizations. There are mutual benefits in these functional exchanges and linkages, as well as the danger that involvement with government can distort their operations, invite an unwelcome regime of external controls, and eventually undermine their independence.

The latter are real possibilities, but they are not inevitable. Voluntary organizations can protect their ability to govern themselves in the interest of their members and avert domination by outsiders or by their own officials (Esman and Uphoff 1984). The defense of full autonomy usually yields to the practical benefits available from engaging in transactions with other voluntary associations at the local level—horizontal linkages—and with organizations that are controlled by government or the private sector— vertical linkages. Through such horizontal and vertical linkages, needed information, resources, and other forms of support are acquired and exchanged.

While defending and maintaining their vital freedom of action, voluntary associations find ways to accommodate to these external linkages, the complexity of these relationships being the price they pay for the benefits they bring. If a farmers' association is to participate in a government-sponsored crop research program from which its members hope to benefit, it must be willing to make available its members' land, labor, skills, and experience with local farming conditions and to accommodate to the routines of the research center; the research center must be similarly prepared to provide the necessary scientific skills and research equipment and to accommodate to the capabilities and convenience of the farmers. Each capitalizes for mutual advantage on what the other is able to contribute.

The management of external linkages is an important responsibility of the leaders of voluntary associations. Despite the temptation to dominate and control the details of programmatic relations with their publics, it is in the interest of government agencies to resist this tendency. Members will no longer participate in or contribute to voluntary organizations that have been subverted, preempted, and reduced to instruments of government patronage and control. They will accept subsidies and services when these are available through such channels, but they will no longer invest their own resources, energies, or loyalties in an organization they identify as government controlled. When this happens, government officials may believe they have eliminated troublesome competitors; in fact, they have displaced actual or potential partners as well as the benefits of voluntary participation, local information, resource contributions, and management. With their limited financial and managerial capabilities, government agencies must then revert to direct administration.

In the choice between autonomy and linkages, the latter, despite the attendant risks and the need to guard against dependency, preemption, or co-optation, is usually the sounder strategy. There is another choice that confronts voluntary organizations: between an emphasis on claim making and an emphasis on self-help. Both are expressions of collective empowerment. Self-help is the process by which groups learn to attend to their collective needs and to solve problems by their own means without relying on outsiders, a source of both collective power and collective pride. Claim making, on the other hand, is an essentially political process by which an organization attempts to extract from outsiders resources, services, or forms of behavior to which it believes it is entitled. Frequently the main target of claim making is government.

Well-placed publics routinely make demands on government for a variety of protections and benefits. Disadvantaged groups tend to feel neglected, deprived, or abused by government and its officials. Organized pressures to rectify these imbalances can be useful, since governments tend to take account of organized demands. Voluntary associations provide the vehicle by which disadvantaged publics can be empowered to make collective claims on governments and its agents that would be impossible for individuals acting alone. Although in many situations this may be productive in increasing the flow of resources and improving the quality of services, claim making may yield limited benefits in LDCs where governments are impecunious, have limited capacities to respond, and are disinclined to yield to societal pressures. Collective self-help, on the other hand, activates energies and resources that have lain dormant and unmobilized; it can produce fresh streams of goods and services that had previously been unavailable. Given the limited capabilities of governments and private enterprises in so many Third World countries, collective self-help should be the dominant motif for voluntary organizations. Claim making becomes most convincing to officialdom after organizations have demonstrated credible performance with collective self-help.

Some voluntary associations originate in the successful experience of grassroots publics that evolve means to meet their collective needs. Some are initiated by more privileged members of society: businesspeople, professionals, religious leaders, and students, both indigenous and foreign. Others may be prompted by government agencies in pursuit of their programmatic goals. Those that are most successful foster self-management by members and methods of governance that reflect members' experience and express their collective preferences rather than using organizational blueprints and management procedures imposed by outsiders, including government. Over time, especially as they expand their activities, voluntary associations may evolve elaborate and sophisticated indigenous patterns of management.

Voluntary associations are, however, vulnerable to gratuitous interference from outsiders, to internal factionalism, and to faulty judgment, deficient skills, and financial abuses by their own leaders and managers. Mistakes due to poor judgment and limited skills can often be overcome by experience, learning, and training, but corruption among leaders can so undermine confidence among rank-and-file members that it destroys the organization. The strongest and most reliable preventative to management abuses is transparency in the organization's transactions, especially financial. This includes the timely publication of accounts, combined with procedures that invite the participation of members in ongoing decisions and periodic election of officers. Voluntary associations seldom succumb to the iron law of oligarchy or to abusive mismanagement as long as they succeed in maintaining their participatory ethos and practices.

Their capacity to handle important and complex economic and welfare activities has been convincingly demonstrated on all continents. Many such latent capacities have, however, been unrealized because of the hostility of governments, their unwillingness to provide needed assistance, or their tendency to encroach on the independence of voluntary associations and thereby undermine the incentives of members to maintain them. Because of the importance of informational and resource exchanges and of vertical linkages, success depends not only on the performance of their leadership but also on the skills of government managers in working with and through the networks provided by voluntary associations. This depends, in turn, on the government's posture toward voluntary collective action—a topic to which I return later in this chapter.

LOCAL AUTHORITIES

In most Third World states, local government is underdeveloped. The "modern" rulers of these polities tend to distrust local elites whose political power based on landed wealth or traditional social status may, they fear, escape their control and serve the ambitions of their political enemies. In the name of national unity, operating efficiency, and modernization, state elites have concentrated and centralized responsibility for public services in the hands of official bureaucracies under their control. These are sometimes supplemented by local political bosses whose power is based on their access to state patronage. Education and public health as well as infrastructural and economic services for agriculture, industry, transportation, power, and even urban and community development have been taken over by central governments. Local administration in the hands of officials of central government bureaucracies has supplanted and stifled responsible local government. Local authorities, some of which had thrived even under colonial regimes, have been reduced to shells (Maddick 1963). The functions they are allowed to perform are strictly circumscribed; their taxing powers are constrained; they cannot afford to hire technically or managerially competent staff. Their operations are strictly supervised and often overridden by administrative "tutelage." A substantial proportion of the meager funds at their disposal is in grants from the central government, and their uses are tightly stipulated and controlled. In some areas, local government simply does not function; such public services as are available are supplied by agencies of the state. When local government continues to function, it is often so impoverished and ineffective that the public holds it in contempt and looks to the central government and its bureaucratic agencies when they need assistance (Mawhood 1983).

The resulting dependency has deprived local communities of the opportunity for responsible self-government, for identifying needs that can be dealt with by local initiative, for evoking local leadership and citizen participation, for raising and managing the required funds, for providing services in ways that respond to local demand, and for regulating the conflicts that inevitably accompany the institutions of self-government. Some local needs are unattended to; others are left to state bureaucracies that often lack the means and the appreciation of specific local conditions to provide useful services. The financial stress that has afflicted so many governments in recent years has, however, begun to produce a reassessment of the potential for local government to mobilize funds and to manage basic services that contribute to quality of life and to economic productivity, but that central governments cannot afford and in any case have difficulty adapting to specific local needs and conditions.

In order to activate local initiative and responsibility, the political and administrative elites of the state will have to revise their basic orientation toward local government. Though local institutions may provide modest political bases for potential opponents and for conservative local elites, the limited range of local government activities and of the patronage available to them need not be construed as threats to the stability of central regimes. Greater latitude for local taxation and revenue enhancement need not threaten the fiscal powers of the state. In societies where collective initiatives and responsibility have been stifled for long periods of time, grassroots initiatives will not necessarily emerge merely because the central government has changed its posture and urged local authorities to be more active. In addition to conceding additional taxing powers and urging local authorities to come to life, the central government may have to provide continuing encouragement and support for local authorities as they undertake a wider range of functions. This should include technical assistance and training facilities for local leaders and employees. Despite their financial stringency, central governments may have to provide incentives in the form of grants in support of ongoing services and of loans for capital improvements to stimulate local efforts. In some lines of activity, the participation of the central government may be contingent on local efforts, both financial and managerial, and subject to the maintenance of standards set by the center. In some cases, there may be clear divisions of labor; in others, shared costs. Local authorities accountable to local publics can thus become more active participants in the financing and management of public services.

Local authorities have much to contribute to improved and expanded services in rural areas and small towns. They can operate and maintain such basic facilities as local roads, water supply systems, schools, health centers, and markets; provide basic sanitary services; and assist small-scale and medium-size industry, including enterprises in the informal sector. Their greater potential, however, is in urban areas (Rondinelli and Cheema 1988). With rapid population growth and intensified rural-urban migration, the rate of urbanization is accelerating in all Third World countries, in many of which a majority of people will live in urban centers by the beginning of the twenty-first century. Population density in urban areas creates imperative needs for services of all sorts—water supply and sanitation, streets, side-walks and lighting, traffic control, police and fire protection, the safety of buildings, sites and services for housing, mass transportation, control of communicable diseases, regulation of land use, and promotion of local economic development. Such activities are normally assigned to local government. The concentration of property and other forms of wealth and the intensity of economic transactions in urban centers produce the potential for tax revenues and user fees that are adequate to finance a significant range of local public services. The demand for such services in urban centers and for their expansion and improvement is inexhaustible. Some, such as education and electric power, may continue to be provided by the central government, though these may be enriched by local contributions. Overall, because of greater visibility, the concentration of demand, and the presence of an articulate middle class, urban residents tend to be much better served by governments than their rural compatriots, an expression of the Third World phenomenon of urban bias (Lipton 1977).

Though local councils may be dominated by businesspeople and politicians, the management of municipal services requires full-time trained staff, some with professional qualifications. They may be compensated at levels comparable to their counterparts working for the central government. The adequacy of municipal services is affected by the revenue sources that local authorities are allowed to tap and by the capabilities and incentives of local managers. Both of these can be favorably influenced by the central government by conceding reasonable sources of taxation and user fees and providing assistance in the training of municipal staff.

Central government elites have been tempted to bring all public services and the revenues needed to finance them under their direct control. This has been the experience of most Third World states, including some that are formally structured along federal lines. This bias in favor of centralization is premised on the values of efficiency and fairness, so that the benefits of scale and superior administration can be realized and services made equally available to all, despite disparities in local economic means. The uniform distribution of services is said to promote political community, nation building, and common allegiance to the state. The aforementioned suspicion of the political motives and loyalties of local elites reinforces the bias toward centralization. The consequences have been unfortunate. Some centrally designed and centrally administered services fail to account for local variability, thereby failing the test of efficiency. They deny to local societies the opportunity and indeed the responsibility to act together to meet their collective needs and deal with their common problems, fostering passivity and dependency rather than active and responsible citizen behavior. When financial and managerial capacities at the center are critically short—and this is now commonplace—it is an especially perverse policy to inhibit the mobilization of resources and of capacities for management that are latent and potentially available at the local level.

Local authorities can take advantage of indigenous voluntary associations to extend the range of a variety of public services (Tendler 1988). Neighborhood associations in municipal areas may demand improved services from hard-pressed city governments, but they can also contribute by their own collective efforts to a variety of services from street maintenance to child health and nutrition programs and volunteer firefighting. To evoke the participation of voluntary associations, local authorities may have to contribute equipment, supplies, and technical staff for ad hoc projects as well as for ongoing services. Municipal management requires cadres of personnel trained and skilled in such fields as finance and accounting, civil and environmental engineering, social work, and law enforcement. Paraprofessional personnel, as described in Chapter 3, can help extend municipal services in cost-effective ways, working where possible with voluntary associations. In addition to routine services, municipal management can foster economic expansion in both the formal and nonformal sectors, generating employment and local revenues.

The case for building up local government, for rescuing it from decades of neglect and deprivation, is in no way the ideological expression of grassroots "localitis," of communitarian populism, or of hostility to the state. The potentials of local authorities are not unlimited but they are substantial, and for the most part these capabilities remain undeveloped. The state will continue to command the more productive tax sources, access to foreign aid, and the ability to borrow. Some services can be more efficiently provided by the center, and others should continue to be managed by the center because of their size, technological complexity, interregional impacts, political sensitivity, or contribution to nation building. Even when functions are devolved to local authorities, the center may set and enforce standards, provide matching funds, or arrange financial transfers that equalize services among areas at different levels of economic development, even when these services are actually managed by local authorities. On the other hand, many activities of government are best performed by local authorities in the interest of efficiency, responsiveness, and democratic control. These functions should be clearly vested in rural or urban local authorities, along with access to needed financial resources. As I have noted, there is much that central governments and sympathetic foreign donors can do to strengthen the institutional capabilities of local governments.

The scale of local authorities, especially in rural areas, should be large enough to permit significant mobilization of resources, but small enough to allow attentive publics to identify with and maintain access to them. One task for development management is to determine which sets of public services are most appropriate for local government, urban and rural, according to the pragmatic criteria of operating efficiency and responsiveness. Overloading local governments with functions that greatly exceed their capabilities is a sure prescription for their breakdown. Provisions must be made for strengthening the institutional capabilities of local authorities, in the absence of which they will continue to languish and default on their new responsibilities. Next must come understandings about divisions of labor and of financial resources, of patterns of intergovernmental cooperation, and of the coproduction and coprovision of public services (see Chapter 6).

INSTITUTIONAL PLURALISM AND THE CONSOLIDATING STATE: CAN THEY COEXIST?

The elites of many Third World states confront societies that contain powerful centrifugal forces, that are poorly integrated economically, that enjoy little sense of cultural or political community, and that identify only vaguely with the symbols and institutions of the state. Consequently, they believe that only through a strong and centralized state apparatus—implemented, if need be, by military or single-party rule that can curb oppositional political expression, dominate the economy, monopolize public services, and limit the scope of autonomous economic and political actors— can the state, from the top-down, begin to shape a sense of common nationhood and move traditional societies toward social modernization and economic development. Once such a statist paradigm or mind-set takes hold, as it did among the political and administrative elites of LDCs in the three decades after World War II, pluralism becomes a threat to these goals and to the elites' control of the polity, including their patronage and privileges. Pluralism becomes a dangerous enemy that needs to be curbed by co-optation, patronage, regulation, denial of resources, and, if necessary, proscription and confiscation. Administrative centralization has been the handmaiden of the monistic state everywhere, even in those polities that tolerate some expressions of economic and political pluralism.

The monistic and highly centralized state has proved to be an impediment to economic development. State control and operation of the economy through official bureaucracies fail to provide incentives for economic efficiency or for responsiveness to consumers. Initiatives and problem-solving capacities within society are systematically stifled as power and resources are monopolized and concentrated within the state apparatus. The absence of public pressure blocks the feedback of information that might correct programmatic and management errors; it provides license for official corruption and perpetuates the incompetent and insensitive provision of public services. In many countries, ambitious and often well-intended efforts by governments to penetrate society with useful public services have been thwarted as the financial capacities of the center have become stressed and its management capabilities overextended. The quiet crisis of centralized and overloaded Third World states has been eclipsed by the dramatic collapse of the economies of Eastern Europe and the Soviet Union, which had been the inspiration for many of the state-managed economies in the Third World. The proof that this light has failed is compelling.

This book is an argument for the necessity and indeed the inevitability of administrative and societal pluralism. Instead of attempting to operate the economy or to monopolize public services, the state should capitalize on the pluralism inherent in all societies, stimulating, cultivating, and tapping every source of initiative that can produce commodities and services of value to society. Embracing pluralism means some sharing of power with organizations outside the state apparatus as well as deconcentrated management within the state's administrative structures. This may be an unwelcome necessity for some Third World elites, but it can be avoided only at very high social cost. Contrary to their conventional zero-sum conviction that the diffusion of initiative and responsibility in society and government will weaken the state and threaten their regimes, the very opposite is more likely to be the case. The relaxation of state controls and the dispersion of economic initiatives and management responsibility are more likely to enhance societal robustness, resilience, and problem-solving performance, the effects of which are to strengthen and stabilize the state. Under a development strategy premised on pragmatic pluralism, the state does not depart the scene; it remains an essential actor. The working presumption, however, is that operational activities that can be devolved to other institutions in society should be released and committed to their control and management.

Not only can the state and institutional pluralism coexist, but the latter actually enhances the former's effectiveness and legitimacy. The sclerosis that afflicts so many overcentralized Third World states confronts their elites with no realistic option but to learn to adjust their patterns of governance to the inevitability and the benefits of institutional pluralism. The issue for the next several decades is whether they handle this necessary adjustment well or poorly. The learning process may be easier for those elites, including many in Latin America, who are accustomed to some legitimate political competition and some autonomous private enterprise than for those in Asia, Africa, and the Middle East who, aspiring to a monistic centralized state, have actively repressed societal pluralism.

This chapter has outlined the main sources of initiative and responsibility that are likely to be present in LDCs with which states can share the burdens and reap the rewards of providing services that are instrumental to economic and social development. In a pluralistic environment, the state continues to control substantial resources and to exercise considerable power, but it must be prepared to accommodate the needs and interests of its nongovernmental partners; otherwise, such partners' initiatives, capabilities, and potentials will shrivel. Conflicts between nongovernmental entities and some elements of government will inevitably arise over a wide range of issues, among them their mutual boundaries and the conditions under which they operate, including tax rates, budget allocations, credit arrangements, and regulatory enforcement. Such disputes are likely to be settled by political give and take, with government and its bureaucracies holding a strong bargaining position. The patterns of sharing responsibility and operations with private enterprise, voluntary associations, and local government may result in a process that has come to be recognized as "coproduction" or "coprovision," in which many units in and out of government contribute to the joint supply of useful goods and services (Ferris 1984). Service networks, the instruments of pluralist administration, are the focus of the next chapter.

The implications of administrative pluralism for development management have begun to be addressed in the literature (White 1989). This development strategy clearly requires the diffusion of management capabilities and skills. Some such abilities are likely to be inherent among businesspeople, local government personnel, and leaders of voluntary associations. These can, however, be enhanced by regimes of incentives and sanctions that reward managers who use resources efficiently, responsibly, and ethically: competitive market discipline plus government regulations for enterprise management; membership control for voluntary associations; public surveillance for local officials. Some management skills can be learned experientially on the job, but others can better be acquired systematically in more formal educational settings. As part of their responsibility for education, governments can provide facilities for management training at all levels, not only for the staffs of government agencies and state enterprises but also for the private business sector, the leaders and employees of voluntary associations, and officials of local authorities. Management training at the academic and practical levels is a favorite of foreign donors, a low-cost contribution to improving resource use in private as well as public institutions that includes the diffusion of knowledge and practices employed in their own societies. Donors are prepared both to provide facilities and to train trainers and management researchers. Management development can also be fostered by professional associations of managers patronized by private enterprise as well as by government; many of them are active in LDCs.

The conventional separation of management education and management development by the private profit-making sector (business schools) and the public-service sector (schools and institutes of public administration) is not a useful approach for Third World countries. This is not, as some argue, because government management, private-enterprise management, and voluntary-association management are essentially identical; actually, the differences—especially in the area of accountability—are very significant. The reason is not so much that some management technologies apply across the board as that the institutional requirements for economic development in Third World countries breach the conventional boundaries between government and business that have characterized the dominant Anglo-American approach to public administration and management education. In LDCs, governments not only operate economic enterprises but they are also involved in policy and investment decisions, in regulatory practices, and in the provision of services that directly affect the environment in which private enterprise must function. Private enterprise must cope not only with market competition but also with government policies and regulations at the macro and micro levels and with opportunities created by government-sponsored promotional and contracting activities. Public-sector managers cannot afford to be illiterate in basic economic analysis or insensitive to the needs of the private or voluntary sectors; nor can private-enterprise managers afford to be innocent of the political and legal context of government operations or of the pressures that drive the behavior of government officials.

Common education and training experiences from the stages of basic skills acquisition to seminars and workshops for senior executives are likely to be far more productive for all participants than segregated learning. Thus by common language, common concepts, and common skills and methods, management education can help to integrate some of the diversity that arises from the structural pluralism outlined in this chapter. Common educational and training experiences can produce informal bonds of friendship that facilitate the cross-institutional problem solving and management cooperation that are addressed in the next chapter.

The most challenging implications of institutional pluralism for development management are not the operations of individual enterprises or government programs, but the shaping and guidance of the service networks that involve the interests and the participation of multiple governmental agencies, business enterprises, voluntary organizations, and local authorities. Having identified in this chapter the parties that make up this pluralistic universe and their potential for releasing energies that contribute to social and economic development, we move to the processes by which these diverse capabilities can be fruitfully combined.[2]

NOTES

[1] Robert Wade (1990) has argued convincingly that the striking economic surge of the "little dragons," Korea and Taiwan, following Japanese precedents, was facilitated by active and sustained state intervention and guidance, well beyond the provision of social and physical infrastructure. While most of their industry has been owned and operated by private firms, governments actively identified potential growth sectors of the economy and deliberately promoted them by policies that channeled capital on favorable terms, socialized risks by such measures as export subsidies, protecting domestic markets, and withdrawing supports when they were no longer needed. Highly competent, growth-oriented, and honest professional bureaucrats managed these activities as agents of the state. Despite vigorously cultivated neoclassical myths, these strategies were more often than not effective in picking winners. Conditions in most Third World countries are seldom conducive to this pattern of state intervention and "governed markets"; for this reason they are not recommended in this book. The experience of the little dragons proves, however, that where conditions are right, internationally competitive private industry can indeed be fostered by policies that require vigorous state intervention.

[2] After this chapter was drafted, I encountered a book whose scope is broader than development management and whose data are drawn only from Africa, but whose approach to development is in many respects congruent with my own (Wunsch and Olowu 1990). Particularly relevant are the chapters written by Professor Olowu, whose orientation can perhaps be summarized in this passage:

> An alternative economic strategy will accept the market critique of the statist strategy, but will address the shortcomings of the market approach highlighted in this chapter. It will address both macro and micro economic policies and institutions, giving special emphasis to the latter. It will recognize that economic reform is basically a political and indeed constitutional issue. *In particular it will recommend a polycentric institutional order comprising a diversity of people-based political and economic organizations. Such organizations will be granted broad latitudes of autonomy to enable them to compete or collaborate with one another and to be self-regulating and accountable.* Within such a framework, a central government with limited but significant functions for promoting appropriate legislation, research, and common services will be required. (Emphasis added.) (p. 123)

6

MULTIORGANIZATIONAL
SERVICE NETWORKS

IN CHAPTER 5 I OUTLINED THE MULTIPLE SOURCES OF INITIATIVE AND ENERGY IN
society outside the family and the household that may be available for
supplying the streams of goods and services needed for social and economic
development. The state, which sets and enforces the terms and conditions
for social order and whose coercive power is justified in modern times as the
instrument of the general will or national interest, need not and should not
be the monopoly supplier of services. Though the shortcomings of large-
scale public bureaucracies can be mitigated and often overcome by methods
such as those surveyed in Chapter 3, the state's limited managerial and
financial capabilities remain as constraints on the performance of the
productive and service activities necessary for economic and social progress.
To overcome the inherent disabilities of the overloaded state, another
development strategy is needed, one that encourages and welcomes the
participation of every sector of society that is potentially capable of generating and managing purposeful action.

A pluralistic development strategy that evokes and relies on multiple
sources of initiative and organized effort must address the question of
relations among them and between them and government. The principle of
division of labor may apply in a rough way to particular domains of activity.
For example, there may be widespread agreement that agricultural production should be in private hands, but that agricultural education, research,
and the diffusion of information should be the responsibility of the state. Or
that the state should construct roads, local authorities should maintain
them, and trucking services should be handled by private firms. Or that the
provision of maternal and child health services should be primarily a
government responsibility, but information and education on family planning might better be left to voluntary organizations, while private dealers
stock and sell contraceptive devices. Such rough divisions of labor may

reflect general understandings of relative efficiency, financial capacity, or political sensitivity. Though some sanctions may be applied effectively by voluntary associations, regulation and accompanying enforcement are generally more appropriate for government. On the other hand, the production of marketable commodities with its premium on flexibility, efficiency, and responsiveness to demand belongs in the private sector. Although such broad principles may be useful as initial premises or points of departure, they cannot account for multiple factors that might modify the division of labor in specific circumstances. These include such considerations as national security and public safety, availability of capital or of competitive enterprise, religious values, and equitable access to essential services.

Clear divisions may evolve and function as guiding principles, but they are often modified at the margin or even fundamentally compromised by competing interests or the practical complexities that accompany economic development. Assume, for example, that central banking needs to be in the hands of the state because the state, as a function of macroeconomic policy, must control the money supply, regulate interest rates, and manage foreign exchange; on the other hand, banking and financial services for the public, though regulated by government, ought to be owned and operated by private firms or voluntary associations, such as credit unions. What if needs emerge, along with political pressures, for production credit to small farmers or export credits to small businesses or mortgages for low-income housing, but these appear too risky and therefore uninteresting to private banks? How might these demands be met within a division of labor such as that outlined above? If the government responds by establishing and operating specialized financial institutions for these purposes or if, instead, it offers loan guarantees for existing private institutions, in effect subsidizing them, then the original division of labor has been breached, or at least modified on the margin. Such practical necessities confound efforts to establish clear divisions of labor in any sector of Third World economies. Instead of clear institutional divisions of labor, what is likely to emerge are complex entanglements involving multiple participants from government, private enterprise, voluntary associations, and local authorities.

Pluralistic strategies of economic development that encourage widespread organizational initiatives are especially prone to such entanglements, to horizontal linkages between them, and to the formation of multiorganizational service networks. Service networks are expedient arrangements in which two or more organizations, usually including governmental as well as nongovernmental actors, participate in the joint production and provision of sets of goods or services. While retaining their original identity, distinctive interests, and autonomous management, participants combine their efforts and contribute their resources toward common objectives in integrated processes of coproduction and coprovision.

Coproduction through service networks has not been unknown in less developed countries (LDCs). Indeed, the proliferation in a dozen countries of complex drug networks involving units of government, local authorities, and private enterprise in the production, processing, and international marketing of narcotics testifies to impressive capacities to form and operate multiorganizational networks when the incentives are sufficient.

As the logical consequence of pluralist patterns of development, service networks are likely to expand and to become the norm for the supply of a wide range of goods and services as economic development intensifies. Indeed, some observers regard networks as the dominant metaorganizations of the future (Naisbett 1982). The managerial implications of service networks that emerge from pluralistic strategies of development are the subject of this chapter.

THE STRUCTURE OF SERVICE NETWORKS

Multi-institutional service networks can be found in all sectors of the economy, and they are associated with each of the major functions of government—regulation, promotion, and services. A familiar example in regulation is the practice of many governments in motor-vehicle inspection: Government specifies safety standards and licenses privately owned garages to perform the actual inspections; government officials periodically inspect the inspectors to enforce standards, while private insurance companies pressure government to set tough standards and licensed garages to enforce them strictly. In promoting housing construction for low- and medium-income families, the state may assist local authorities by clearing land; providing basic highway, water, and sewage facilities; and making subsidies available to private financial institutions for low-interest mortgages or loans to assist with self-help construction by members of local cooperatives. A multiorganizational network of this kind may involve one or more units of the central government as the promoter and the provider of subsidies, local authorities as the contributors of sites and infrastructure, private banks as the source of mortgage financing, construction companies as suppliers of building materials, and self-help housing cooperatives. The coordination of these diverse contributions from several autonomous providers requires structures, and these structures must be managed.

The most common networks are those that produce and deliver social and economic services. A simple example relates to electric power. A government corporation may be the monopoly generator of electricity, but it may share the burden of distribution to individual industrial, commercial, and household consumers with municipally owned companies, private profit-seeking firms, or rural electrification cooperatives, while government regulates rates and requires that private accounting firms audit the books of the participating units. Similarly in irrigation, government may build and operate the large dams and main channels, serving as wholesaler to water-user associations, which are self-managed voluntary organizations of farm-ers that control the flow of water to individual holdings, maintain the secondary and tertiary channels by their own labor or by hiring private contractors, and collect the fees required to operate and maintain the system and pay the government's water rates. Together these horizontal linkages constitute complex and sophisticated management systems or networks.

Elaborating further on this theme, consider the activity of agricultural production. Owner-cultivators may belong to a self-managed cooperative that owns and operates its own trucks and processing facilities; borrows funds for production credit from a government-operated credit institution; buys its production inputs wholesale from private suppliers and then retails them to its members; relies on government agencies for applied research, extension, and plant protection services; and markets its crops and livestock through private dealers who also handle postharvest processing and storage. There are a number of alternative mixes of responsibilities in complex networks of this kind. They may involve several government agencies and several competing private firms as well as voluntary associa-tions at the basic and federated levels. Prices, in this example, may be set by market forces, but the example would be more complex if the government were also involved in fixing and enforcing prices or providing subsidies for either production inputs or marketed crops. In no other sector are service networks as dense and as varied as in agricultural production and marketing.

For an illustration in the social sector, take the field of public health. In LDCs, ministries of health are likely to be in charge of epidemiological activities; to license and certify public-health workers; to operate general hospitals and outpatient clinics; and to sponsor, help finance, and supply community health facilities. Government agencies at the central or provin-cial level may also provide some services related to nutrition and family planning. The health field attracts the interest of voluntary associations, foreign and domestic, which may participate in all but the regulatory phases of medical and health activities, particularly in public information, clinical care (especially for children), and assistance to local and community facili-ties. Governments may make their assistance to community health services contingent on the provision and maintenance of buildings by local authori-ties and their participation in selecting and compensating paraprofessional health workers, while their training and supervision remain government responsibilities. Local authorities may also be expected to furnish equip-ment and labor to assist in the implementation of environmental sanitation measures. Local women's and other user associations may be needed to help manage local health centers and to participate in nutritional, child health, and family-planning activities; they may share responsibility for health education, which also involves local schools and government-operated or private mass media. Although the government may employ many medical and health practitioners, other private health providers may be engaged part time on a contract basis; some services, such as midwifery, may be provided privately, but in government facilities. Government may contract with private firms for the supply and delivery of pharmaceuticals and hospital supplies and equipment.

In the three decades following World War II, governments moved aggressively into the health field in response to public demand and the pressures of foreign donor agencies. The need and the demand have overwhelmed the professional, financial, and managerial capabilities of governments and induced them to welcome the participation of voluntary agencies, community associations, local authorities, and private providers and suppliers. When a variety of organizations participates in each of the several branches of health administration, a series of networks emerges. In each of them, responsibilities are distributed while financial and personnel contributions are coordinated among two or more organized participants so that needed services can be coprovided through their joint efforts. Conflicts inevitably surface because each of the participants retains its distinctive orientation and point of view on health care, has its own organizational interests to promote and protect, and manages its own affairs. Some of them may be supported morally and financially by domestic interest groups and by foreign donors.

The continuing viability of its component units is essential, but the outputs of the network surpass the sum of its parts. Keeping the various health networks operating by adjusting to changing conditions, reconciling disputes, and establishing and maintaining workable modus vivendi is the continuing task of managers of all the participating agencies. This burden is shared, however, by development managers or network facilitators at the coordinating levels of government.

HOW SERVICE NETWORKS ARE SHAPED

Service networks originate in two ways: by spontaneous accommodation and by government policy.

Spontaneous accommodation is the process by which organizations find it convenient to establish relationships and form linkages with others performing related functions rather than attempt to expand their own activities into areas already occupied by others. An agricultural cooperative has the choice, in principle, of performing some of its own research or relying on existing research agencies, particularly those in government, but exerting influence to orient the government's research resources to the needs and priorities of its members. As mutual dependency evolves, the elements of a network are formed. The same cooperative society may face similar choices in the areas of processing and marketing. It may rely on existing organizations in the private sector for one or both of these services, or its members may decide that they can do better by operating their own processing facilities and developing their own marketing channels, eliminating the middleman. The cooperative may seek financing for its expansion from a government-owned agricultural bank. By expanding its operations through vertical integration, it may reduce its linkage relationships and its dependency on outsiders, but at the price of greater internal complexity; by relying on government credit, it forms new linkages and dependencies, but reduces its risks and simplifies its managerial tasks.

In the generation following independence, many governments in LDCs invaded fields of activity previously performed—though often with limited range and limited effectiveness—by nongovernmental organizations and incorporated these activities into monopolistic state bureaucracies. Instead of working with and through existing nongovernmental organizations, attempting to strengthen them, encouraging them to expand into related services, and linking them into multi-institutional structures, governments instead weakened, displaced, and even destroyed them. The result was that once capabilities and initiatives outside government had been impaired or stifled, government found that it could not command the managerial skills or financial resources needed to mount adequate services entirely on its own and that bureaucratic monopolies lacked the incentives and the flexibility required for efficiency and responsiveness. As a result of this costly learning process, governments have been changing course, accepting and even inviting participation by nongovernmental actors. While retaining many functions in their own bureaucracies, they have improvised service networks as the main instrument for coordinating those activities that governments now share with organizations outside their ranks.

Many networks continue to be shaped because organizations, including government agencies, find it convenient to stay in their specialized niches or lack the realistic possibility of diversifying. This is entirely consistent with the trend toward organizational specialization and differentiation that accompanies modernization and economic development (Durkheim 1933). Specialization and differentiation create the need for integration, the function performed by service networks. By processes of mutual accommodation and sometimes of deliberate negotiation, interorganizational understandings are improvised. These arrangements—sometimes tacit, sometimes formal—regulate the terms and conditions of membership in service networks that involve multiple participants. Although each participating organization continues to concentrate on its specialized functions and to defend its boundaries, all of them recognize that their activities alone would be sterile except for the complementary contributions of others. This interdependency cannot, however, be random. It must be ordered and structured. This is the logic of coproduction and of the necessity for service networks.

There is a continuum among service networks. At one extreme are those that are shaped primarily by government initiative, on the other those that evolve primarily by mutual accommodation. Those that include a prominent regulatory component such as motor-vehicle inspection lie close to the government-initiated pole and are more likely to experience government intervention; those oriented to service, such as family-planning networks, lie closer to the mutual accommodation/self-organizing end of the spectrum and are likely to enjoy greater autonomy. Even when service networks are formed, adjusted, and readjusted by mutual accommodation among the parties, a strategy of pluralistic development entails a supportive posture and policy regime on the part of government. Public policy in support of service networks should incorporate these four elements:

1. Identifying and facilitating the development of organizational capabilities outside government in the private profit-seeking sector, in community and voluntary associations, and among local authorities. Activating them may require more than general encouragement; specific positive inducements may be needed, such as expanding their legal power to raise revenues, which enables local authorities to undertake additional functions.

2. Creating incentives for new actors to organize and participate in the production of goods and services. This is especially useful for smaller private firms and for voluntary associations with limited experience and modest resources. Technical assistance and training in production, marketing, and management methods; sources of credit; and access to complementary services on nondiscriminatory terms may help them prosper and become useful contributors to service networks.

3. Withdrawing or reducing government participation in operational activities when alternative organizations demonstrate interest and competence, for example, in the marketing of fertilizer or the operation of passenger transport services. Having fostered the growth of rural electrification cooperatives, having offered voluntary organizations a major role in the distribution of contraceptive devices, the state can reduce its participation in these activities or pull out entirely. The state's withdrawal from operations goes beyond privatization as that concept is conventionally understood, for it devolves activities to voluntary associations and local authorities as well as to private firms.

4. Intervening to smooth and facilitate the linkage process and to promote and protect the goals of public policy, but deferring whenever
   possible to self-adjusting processes within the networks. This may
   involve helping the parties, including government bureaus and
   parastatals, to fill gaps in the networks, leaning on some units to
   expand or improve their contributions, even inviting new participants
   into the networks, and mediating conflicts among member organizations. The state thus retains a residual responsibility to ensure the
   viability of service networks. Decisions to intervene are, however,
   judgmental and vulnerable to human error. Government intervention
   may be, or at least be perceived as, politically motivated, favoring some
   parties over others. The consequences cannot be fully predicted, and
   they are not trouble free.

Governments need not be satisfied with waiting for organizations to come
to the fore. Legal, financial, and administrative means can be used and
regulations can be modified in support of market incentives and community pressures to attract and facilitate the emergence and activation of
nongovernment organizations, to expand the range of their services, and to
attract their participation in the networks. Government agencies may also
be targets of such inducements and pressures. In pursuit of a strategy of
pluralistic development, initiatives in the formation and strengthening of
service networks by self-organization and mutual accommodation should
be encouraged. The state cannot, however, abandon its responsibilities for
ensuring the provision of essential services even when most of the actual
providers—members of the networks—are outside government. The vital
entrepreneurial and facilitative functions needed to ensure the continuity of
essential services are entrusted to and supervised by agents of government,
specifically senior development managers.

HOW SERVICE NETWORKS ARE MANAGED

Some of the management implications of service networks are summarized
by Foley (1989), following Gerlach and Hine (1970):

> Networks are decentralized organizations where decision making
> and power are distributed. Networks are coordinated, not controlled.
> Unlike a bureaucracy, there are no centralized planning or adminis-
> trative units. While there is usually a central clearing house or central
> administrative office in a network organization, the other units are not
> dependent on the center. Rather, all the units are flexibly connected.
> Keeping the network functioning, there must be a value consensus,
> collaborative and cooperative behavior, and leadership skills for
> facilitation. (p. 56)

Thus, the contrasting management principles of bureaucratic hierarchy within the components of the network and of flexible coordination between the components must coexist if the networks are to function.

When they emerge from the interests and the needs of their participants, networks can be said to be self-organizing and self-managed. What binds the parties in service networks may be common values, but it is more likely to be sheer practical mutual advantage. Through bargaining and mutual accommodation, the participating organizations arrive at procedures and routines for providing and exchanging information and material resources and for resolving the conflicts that enable networks to function. Such arrangements are entirely consensual. They are perceived by the participants as satisfying their basic interests, given the practical alternatives available to them. Their interests may not be satisfied maximally, but sufficiently to justify continuing participation.

If this were not the case, they might be tempted to withdraw. Private enterprises will stay in a network only as long as the arrangements yield profits, and profitability may be affected by many factors, including changing market conditions. Stresses and conflicts among the participants are certain to occur as each may respond to pressures outside the network in ways that impact unfavorably on their partners. The processes of adjustment are abetted, however, by each participant's understanding that other parties may seek alternative arrangements if they believe their legitimate interests are being disregarded. Thus in the agricultural production example, if a farmers' association believes a private-sector supplier or consortium of suppliers is overcharging or delivering inferior materials, it can terminate the arrangement and look for alternatives, including the handling of procurement on its own. If the government research station finds that the farmers' co-op is not living up to the terms of their agreement, is not contributing its share of land, labor, or other costs, it may decide to abandon the network.

The prospective collapse of ongoing networks in response to such conflicts is likely to entail costs to participating organizations, costs that can be avoided by timely readjustment and renegotiation of the terms of interorganizational linkages. These inevitable stresses ensure that if a multiorganizational service network is to survive, it must be a dynamic, adaptive learning system. Self-managed networks are robust in that they are useful to all the participating organizations and can normally work out consensual adjustments to problems that arise; they are fragile in that they can be disrupted by the self-regarding acts of individual participants whose contributions cannot easily be replaced. Their maintenance and sustainability require that the various parties take account of the needs and interests of fellow participants.

When this fails, a network may collapse and new ones may or may not be formed. Collapse may penalize the public, which suffers the loss or deterioration of services. Since these networks represent a valuable form of social capital, their disintegration and disappearance become a proper concern of government, as pluralistic development strategies rely on them for the implementation of important dimensions of public policy. Governments committed to that strategy cannot afford to adopt an ideologically laissez-faire or hands-off posture toward them. But neither can they afford to command or manipulate them by heavy-handed intervention. This implies that governments may help to shape and maintain them; set broad policy parameters for their activities, especially for the government agencies that participate in the networks; facilitate their adaptation to changing conditions and opportunities; and help to mediate their conflicts. Although a network "may be unlikely to . . . maintain a reasonable level of felt responsibility" among its components, data from several cases "suggest how allegiance to a larger whole may be influenced by those who tie networks together and keep them functioning" (O'Toole 1985, p. 217).

The facilitation and monitoring of these networks is a major function and responsibility of development managers in government, especially of those in senior management or coordinating positions who are not in direct charge of individual agencies. The effectiveness of the networks is probably more important to government policy in support of social and economic development than the performance of individual government agencies. Such agencies need to be efficient and responsive, but they are mainly instrumental to larger policy objectives; increasingly, government policies are implemented through multiorganizational service networks. Thus agricultural research and extension are useful as they contribute to the policy goals of increasing the productivity of land and labor among rural cultivators and raising their levels of well-being; government-operated hospitals are important as components of networks that raise health standards in the areas they serve. Their outputs have limited utility in themselves, unless they are conjoined with the related outputs of cognate organizations. Such examples of coproduction and coprovision can be multiplied and applied to every development-oriented policy that governments sponsor. The network, the system, is more important than the sum of its components.

Since development goals depend on the viability of these networks, governments need to make provision for them: to facilitate their formation, operation, maintenance, and adjustment to changes. Yet governments have been slow to regard the networks that implement their policies, rather than individual agencies or programs, as central to their concerns or as claimants on their executive energy or their finances. They have been slow to establish and staff positions at senior management levels charged with overseeing and supporting the service networks that are critical to their development strategies. This is a lag that will have to be overcome, especially in regimes committed to pluralistic patterns of development. The responsibility to oversee and facilitate the networks will have to be assigned, in many instances on a full-time basis, to managers at coordinating levels in the capital city and in the field. They should be responsible for keeping informed of the ways the networks are performing and for intervening as bureaucratic facilitators or honest brokers when problems arise. Program managers should be evaluated not only by their operating efficiency and their effectiveness in turning out goods and services, but also by their success in working compatibly as members of multi-institutional networks.

The resources available to development managers who intervene to shape or maintain these networks and to settle conflicts among participants are their brokerage and persuasive abilities, the economic incentives at the disposal of government, and their access to senior administrators and influential politicians. Their most important resource is their diplomatic skill, the sense of when to intervene and when to stay out, when to lean hard and when to relax. Another is their ability to reconcile the differing interests of participating organizations in the context of incremental and at times turbulent changes that may affect the resource endowments, opportunities, incentives, and perceptions of the participating parties in different ways. Working within this framework, government managers who facilitate and oversee these networks need to be effective negotiators and problem solvers. Such perspectives and skills should be emphasized in their training and in the criteria by which their performance is evaluated and rewarded.

While bureaucratic structures tend to value stability, service networks are inherently dynamic. The participating units have their own interests, which they do not hesitate to express and promote. As changing circumstances create fresh opportunities, some of them may perceive what appear to be more satisfactory or more profitable alternatives outside the networks. Those with the least flexibility are the government bureaucracies whose responsibilities are mandated by law and policy; unable to withdraw from the networks, they tend to extend their control in the sector in which they operate, thereby enhancing stability while reducing the need to accommodate to others. A pluralistic strategy of development combined with government's chronic financial limitations make full control unattainable and compel the participation of government agencies in multi-institutional networks. The legal and financial weight of the state helps to maintain the bargaining power of government bureaucracies and compensates in some measure for their lesser freedom to withdraw.

Thus it is not only changing circumstances but the continuing strains of multiunit cooperation that produce the dynamism characteristic of service networks. The management of the networks should feature a positive style oriented to anticipating and resolving problems by timely negotiation, combined with the ability to tolerate some ambiguities and allow the parties involved to work out their own differences, so long as these agreements do not transgress law and public policy and are not incompatible with the needs of the network as a system. In overseeing service networks, development managers should be active but not intrusive; they cannot allow incipient problems to go unattended, but they must allow the participants as much latitude as possible to work out fresh accommodations on their own and indeed facilitate that process.

This process of network management is complicated and sophisticated because of the need to broker agreements and reconcile the not entirely consistent needs, priorities, interests, and expectations of the participating units, which may have their own alternatives and resources—among them political support—that they do not hesitate to invoke. Senior managers of the participating units, including government agencies, while producing services and protecting the interests of their own organizations, must at the same time take into account the needs of other parties in the network. In so doing they may be constrained by the policies and bureaucratic practices of their own organizations, which they may nevertheless attempt to bend—while formally complying—in the face of the practical need for flexible accommodation within the structures of the network.

Managers responsible for shaping, coordinating, and maintaining service networks have access to some material resources, notably their ability to affect the flow of public funds; they may also be able to threaten unwanted changes in the regulatory regime if strains within the network cannot be satisfactorily resolved. The interests of the consuming public may be invoked by development managers as a weapon to help discipline unruly members of the networks. The practice of mapping their environment—of identifying and tracing the probable intentions and actions of the various organizations that are relevant to their own mission and the probable reactions of other organizations to their initiatives—is, as described in Chapter 4, a skill that needs to be perfected by development managers responsible for overseeing service networks (White 1990). In this way, they can limit surprises and enjoy a sounder informational base for designing their own tactics and, specifically, for the exercise of the diplomatic skills by which they attempt to reconcile the particularistic interests of the participating organizations with the broader societal purposes embodied in the networks. This is a far cry from the conventional role and image of government managers bound by rigid rules and operating by command in hierarchical structures.

Overseeing the networks is inescapably a managerial responsibility of the state. Officials charged with this function in ministerial or departmental headquarters should be assigned full time to these tasks as facilitators and troubleshooters with direct access to the senior managers of the participating agencies. In the field, where the scale of operations permits, network management may require full-time attention, for example in the governor's office at the province level. This function may be carried out part time by generalist officials in the field, such as district officers who are responsible for overseeing and coordinating all government programs in their territory. Such officials can be specifically charged with the monitoring and maintenance of service networks in the regions for which they are responsible. This, it should be noted, represents an expansion in their conventional coordinating roles, encompassing as it does the activities not only of government agencies but of voluntary associations and private businesses as well.

Managers concerned with service networks must spend much of their time away from their desks and outside the capital city, attempting to form new combinations or to resolve the interorganizational strains that arise among government agencies, including parastatals, and between them and nongovernmental participants. These issues may require revisions in government regulations, policies, budget allocations, staff assignments, and even in laws—as well as in the behavior of nongovernment organizations. The maintenance of the networks and the management and adjustment of the disputes that arise can usually be handled by the participants themselves. The managers from government should stay on the sidelines until it is clear that their intervention is needed.

As the requirements for success in these entrepreneurial and brokerage roles differ markedly from those of conventional program management or bureaucratic leadership within a single agency, persons should be selected whose previous performance has demonstrated qualities such as the capacity to cope with ambiguity and complexity, the patience to withhold action until it is needed, the ability to establish trust and confidence among persons representing organizations with diverse interests, and the ability to reconcile their particularistic interests with broader societal needs represented by the networks. Such skills are frequently not present among successful program managers operating in bureaucratic settings. Before undertaking such responsibilities, persons selected for this role would normally benefit from special training, probably in executive development workshops oriented to these tasks, in which senior persons from the voluntary and private sectors, as well as government line managers, participate. Their performance evaluations and career rewards should take full account of the distinctive responsibilities of network management.

The practical consequences of a pluralistic strategy of development require the implementation of development policies and programs through service networks. The appropriate strategy is to encourage the development of resource mobilizing and operational capabilities outside government in all sectors of society. As these capabilities become manifest, the state should gradually sluff off direct operations, devolve them to nongovernmental organizations, and concentrate increasingly on policy concerns, standards setting, regulation, the diffusion of useful information, and the monitoring of performance. Though this approach represents a far-reaching shift in emphasis, it in no way implies the abandonment of government responsibility for the promotion and guidance of social and economic development. The responsibilities remain, but they are pursued by more appropriate means that draw on powerful but hitherto latent capabilities and resources in society. Many programs will continue to be directly financed and provided by government agencies, but most will be coproduced and coprovided with nongovernment actors. The instrumentalities for this sharing are the multiorganizational networks that become important resources and, in turn, produce new roles that demand more sophisticated skills among development managers.

SERVICE NETWORKS AND SYSTEMS THEORY

Service networks as outlined in this chapter are a species of the "governance networks" discussed by Hult and Walcott (1990). These authors trace the provenance of interorganizational networks and related systems concepts as they have emerged in organization theory, for example, in the work of Charles Perrow (1986). Although their data are drawn entirely from U.S. experience, their theory about interorganizational networks as political structures operating in discrete policy arenas is akin to the concepts and the processes outlined in this chapter. What this chapter attempts is to apply the logic of multistructural networks to LDCs and to demonstrate the important contribution of public development managers to the operation and maintenance of these systems.

The concept of multi-institutional service networks is an expression of the underlying logic of systems structures and processes (Churchman 1968). Systems theories in the social sciences have produced a vast literature, ranging from concrete to highly abstract to even mathematical formulations, to the point that systems constructs purporting to deal with organizational behavior have become as heterogeneous as they are commonplace. Nevertheless, a few key concepts and properties seem to be included in all social systems paradigms: Systems are made up of plural components; the behavior of each has implications for all the others as well as for the system as a whole; communications and transactions among them are more important than the internal behavior of individual components; and the system's performance is greater than the combined outputs of its members. Within this general framework, some systems are "closed" and governed by deterministic and predictable relationships. Others are "open" to outside influences; their internal relationships are in some measure contingent, allowing for considerable degrees of freedom, for the exercise of human will, and therefore for politics. Some are perceived to function like friction-less machines, following mechanistic or architectural principles, others like living creatures inspired by organic metaphors.

Some social systems are conceived as teleological, goal-seeking struc-tures, oriented to purposeful action. Some are macrosocietal and essentially descriptive; others are closer to the realm of human action. Among the latter that touch the role of development managers are sets of interrelated, complex structures that have to be integrated, coordinated, or steered by central command and control. This has been the dominant construct in systems thinking that applies to purposive organizational behavior, pre-scribing for top management the function of integrating by command the system's various components (Vickers 1973). More recently, however, there has emerged the antithetical, bottom-up perspective of self-organizing and self-managing systems that dispense with and indeed reject central guid-ance and control (Jantsch 1980). This perspective emphasizes instead the creative initiatives and adaptive problem-solving capacities inherent in the component actors to form, operate, and maintain complex systems of action. According to this perspective, only self-organizing and self-man-aged methods can generate the energies and process the information needed for the effective and timely governance of complex, purposive systems of action.

The conception and description of service networks in this chapter are inspired by the insights of a pluralistic universe that underlie the bottom-up notion of self-organizing structures and processes. This is not, however, a pure application or extension of the self-organizing paradigm. In the context of Third World development, governments remain responsible for shaping legal regimes and policy frameworks for all the major sectors of development and for striving to implement them through financial alloca-tions, regulations, promotional activities, and the provision of services. In a pluralistic strategy of development, the state recognizes, encourages, and welcomes initiatives from all segments of society. The channeling of these autonomous initiatives can, however, be influenced by law, public policies, and concrete promotional and supportive actions of government; yet the dynamism of these initiatives depends on according them wide latitude to pursue their own organizational goals and cope with their conflicts in the complex and uncertain environments they encounter. The guiding pre-sumption is that the state respects their operating autonomy but is prepared to exert its power when needed to protect an overriding public interest. The principal theoretical weakness of the self-organizing paradigm is its failure to recognize and to come to terms with the reality and indeed the necessity of power, including state power, in societal relationships. That deficiency is overcome in this formulation—at some cost to the simplicity and elegance of the voluntaristic self-organizing paradigm—by ascribing to the state a legitimate, if bounded, role in purposive development processes.

When service networks emerge as a consequence of autonomous initiatives that may involve government agencies as well as nongovernment actors, the role of the state is mainly facilitative. But governments may also participate more actively in the formation of networks when the need or opportunity is evident and missing ingredients (resources or energies) or resistance by some participating organizations seem to block their emergence. This is an appropriate role for the state in the framework of a pluralistic development strategy, as long as it respects the autonomy of the various participants and avoids the temptation to subject them to coercive manipulation or control in the execution of an outsider's design. The presumption concerning the self-limiting behavior of the state cannot be absolute if the consequences of abstention threaten to be socially destructive.

Thus the necessary presence of the state constrains the applicability of the paradigm of self-organizing systems to the concrete service networks described in this chapter. That agents of the state may participate as bureaucratic entrepreneurs in the shaping of organizational networks, facilitate their operation, and help them to manage conflicts modifies the theory to account for contextual realities inherent in Third World development, including ignorance and even perversity among some organizational actors. In its spirit, however, this modified paradigm is far more compatible with the logic of self-organizing systems than with the conventional image of systems of action commanded, controlled, and steered by a central authority. But since the exercise of power may have disruptive as well as beneficent consequences that cannot be foreseen, there can be no guarantee that well-intended but inept interventions by agents of the state may not in some cases undermine the performance of service networks. In these as in all human affairs there are risks.

In this pattern of organization and management, readers may be confused by what might appear to be conflicting roles visualized for the state and its agents: Its service-providing units are members of societal networks, while senior government executives act as promoters, facilitators, and conflict managers of these same networks in which nongovernment as well as government agencies participate. This confusion is a residue of naive monistic images of the state. The reality is that contemporary states are pluralistic structures: Each of its bureaucratic agencies, as I indicated in Chapter 2, has its distinctive resources, publics, powers, and culture; in their daily operations they tend to be loosely integrated and to function with a large measure of autonomy. It is quite possible, therefore, for a cadre of senior government managers in coordinating roles to coexist with other government managers in charge of line operations. These distinct roles for different representatives of government are entirely consistent with the

pluralistic character of contemporary states and with pluralistic development strategies that require the participation of nongovernment organizations along with government agencies. Operating managers are, however,
more likely to accept as legitimate the intermediary role of the facilitator if
that role is reinforced by government doctrine and by sets of incentives and
sanctions that encourage and reward performance-oriented participation
in multiorganizational systems.

Skeptics might also challenge the ability of senior government officials to
function in the facilitative and mediatory roles visualized in this chapter.
Will the nongovernmental participants accept them in these capacities? As
agents of government they necessarily have their agendas—to implement
government policies and programs and even promote narrow political
interests when these are espoused by the government of the day. Therefore,
they cannot always be neutral in dealing with the parties in networks; nor
can they be perceived as entirely fair and impartial by participating organizations, many of whose managers may be highly suspicious of government
and of the motives of its agents. That this negative scenario represents a real
risk cannot be denied; more likely, however, it is overdrawn. Many government agents perform useful intermediary functions even when they are
responsible for implementing government policy, because the policy itself
mandates these brokerage activities. Institutionalizing this role will not
automatically accompany the emergence and expansion of service networks. For this, governments must make specific provision—establish the
positions, train their incumbents, and endow them with the authority and
incentives that legitimate their roles and enable them to perform as facilitators of networks that include, among others, line managers of government
agencies.

DEVELOPMENT MANAGEMENT
AND INSTITUTION BUILDING

For three decades, students and practitioners of development management have been concerned with institution building or institutional
development (Esman 1972b; Israel 1987; Blase 1986). In this section, I limit
myself to summarizing the key concepts and the underlying logic of the
institution-building paradigm, with particular emphasis on its relevance
to multiorganizational service networks.

Although the concept of "institution" has many meanings both in social
science discourse and in everyday usage, among most specialists in Third
World development it refers to organized capacities oriented to socially
sanctioned values. At the core of the concept is organization, based on the
recognition that only through structures of action that combine diverse

human talents and material resources can disciplined and reliable capabilities be mobilized and sustained to perform developmental tasks in all sectors of society. Organizations are basic, but organizations do not become institutions until they are perceived within their own ranks and among relevant publics as embodying norms of behavior and serving values that are widely respected in society.

The abstract values to which societies aspire achieve concrete expression in organizations and their activities; organizations, in turn, gain institutional status and the respect and strength that this conveys only when they appear to be instrumental to valued social purposes. An agricultural research center must first develop the technical and managerial capacities to turn out and disseminate solid and reliable research information. The societal value that it represents is the application of scientific skills and knowledge to the practical needs of ordinary farmers, thereby democratizing scientific information and methods. As a producer of research information, it is an organization with technical capacities. It does not achieve institutional status, however, until it is recognized and respected by relevant publics, especially farmers, as a reliable and continuing source of useful information and practices addressed to their specific needs. It is thus that an organization becomes an institution. Institutional status, in turn, protects the organization's autonomy and facilitates its access to resources.

Values and norms remain abstract aspirations until they are implemented by concrete organizations with the ability to mobilize resources and convert them to outputs that are instrumental to such values. The abstract norms of private economic enterprise, for example, cannot be institutionalized, cannot gain practical and secure expression, until they are embodied in legal codes that protect private property, in courts that enforce contracts, in agencies that maintain competitive markets, in banks that supply credit, and in the firms that actually produce and market goods and services. Institutionality combines organizational competence, productive interorganizational linkages, and societal respect reinforced by supportive public constituencies. Over time, however, institutionalized organizations may fail to innovate or to adapt to changing needs and circumstances; they may even become corrupted. As obstacles to further development, they may be compelled to adapt or reform or face the loss of their constituencies and of their institutional status. The process of displacement may entail considerable tension and struggle. Deinstitutionalization has been the fate, for example, of cooperative organizations in several LDCs.

The organizational capacities that need to be cultivated and strengthened occur in all the productive and human services activities that are instrumental to development. They involve all sectors of society—government, private firms, and voluntary associations. The original investigations into institution building emphasized governmental entities because they were initiated and sponsored by scholars interested primarily in public administration and higher education, which are mostly in the hands of the state. This initial bias has long since been corrected, with increased recognition of the limitations of government and the importance of organizational performance in voluntary associations and in private business (Uphoff 1986b). A pluralistic strategy of development requires the strengthening of organizations and the enhancement of institutional capacities throughout society.

The early research on institution building also focused on individual organizations, on such factors as their leadership, doctrine or guiding philosophy, internal structures and processes, resource mobilization, program outputs, and especially external linkages with other organizations (Esman 1972b). It analyzed the challenges to leadership in addressing simultaneously the need to produce useful services while strengthening capacities for action and the tensions and trade-offs between these competing objectives. It also focused on the dual dimensions of management: the internal, which draws on established management skills, and the interorganizational, which requires more political skills and less familiar methods such as environmental mapping. The emphasis was on process, on the management methods and tactics needed to strengthen organizational capabilities, and especially on the learning and political dimensions of interorganizational relations.

Development-oriented institutions, by definition, introduce change into society; they are agents of purposeful change. Because change may pose threats to some individuals and groups who are not without resources of their own, the intended change and the organizations that promote it may be resisted. At the same time that it sponsors and symbolizes change, management must accommodate existing societal forces in order to ensure access to resources, acceptance of its outputs, and sometimes even survival. The choice of priorities and tactics by which this essentially political process is pursued by organizational leaders, while simultaneously producing and marketing useful outputs and strengthening their internal capacities for action, remains the principal challenge to managers responsible for promoting institutional development.

This process was originally conceived as a management-intensive, top-down exercise in social engineering; indeed the "steering" metaphor was often employed to describe it. In more recent thinking, the learning and political dimensions have been retained, but the elitist, top-down orientation has been supplanted, in belated recognition of the creative initiatives that are present and must be tapped throughout society. Institutions need to be built, but the process involves a wide range of initiatives and participants, including, but not limited to, senior managers. It involves collective efforts throughout society, in the voluntary and enterprise sectors as well as in government. And it focuses increasingly on networks and multiorganizational systems of action as well as on individual organizations. Thus the institution-building paradigm, while retaining and deepening its core insights, has itself evolved through a learning process.

Although individual organizations and the programs for which they are responsible remain the central components and the main units of action for most development managers, the focus of institution building has expanded to incorporate multi-institutional networks. The ultimate effectiveness of individual organizations is tied to larger structures, the networks that integrate their contributions in the process of coproduction with those of complementary organizations. Therefore, institution building, without neglecting the viability of component units, must at the same time transcend them and focus on the more complex and demanding processes of shaping and maintaining multiorganizational networks, relying when possible on the self-organizing capacities of the participants. Greater than the sum of their parts, the networks represent organizational investments and assets that can be replaced only at high cost. With increasing organizational specialization and differentiation, the networks become systems for integrating the specialized efforts of their components.

Thus the logic of institution building can be extended directly to service networks. They too need to be cultivated and managed, because they seldom emerge or survive entirely by spontaneous accommodation. The joint objectives of capacity and institutionality—the latter earned by performance that subserves societal values beyond their instrumental outputs—continue to provide the focus for institution-building activities whether they involve networks or only individual organizations. But while managers in the component units must be concerned with both internal processes and external linkages, managers responsible for the networks are occupied mainly with maintaining compatibility among the participating parties and adjusting to dynamic changes originating within the network or outside. They have little power and usually less inclination to intervene directly in the internal affairs of the autonomous component units. While they are coping with immediate needs associated with providing services, mediating conflicts, and responding to external demands, development managers cannot lose sight of larger objectives—including the long-term viability of service networks as adaptive, change-producing, and change-protecting institutions.

7

ENHANCING MANAGEMENT PERFORMANCE

IN EARLIER CHAPTERS, I MADE THE CASE THAT THE SCOPE OF DEVELOPMENT management extends far beyond conventional public administration. Organizations are central to development management because of their ability to mobilize substantial resources and diverse skills and to guide action on a large and consequential scale. But the significant organizations are not confined to government; they are diffused throughout society. Even under the most favorable conditions, the state alone cannot command sufficient resources, capabilities, or incentives to move societies toward sustained development. Failure to recognize these inherent limitations was the critical mistake of Stalin and his successors in the economic sphere, a mistake that has been repeated again and again by statist elites in Third World countries.

As an expression of the dialectic between state and society, development requires pluralistic strategies that foster complementary enterprise, initiatives, and problem-solving behavior in private businesses, in local governments, and in voluntary associations. The state should encourage—indeed, provide incentives for—nongovernmental organizations to seize the opportunities and assume the burdens of producing and distributing useful goods and services. Where feasible, nongovernmental organizations should be free to operate autonomously under a regime of law to which they are accountable. Many services, however, require the combined efforts of several governmental and nongovernmental organizations in complex patterns of service networks. The shaping and nurturing of these multiorganizational networks, in which the state remains an important participant, are the main challenges to the present generation of development managers.

POINTS OF INTERVENTION

Over time, management systems have emerged in all Third World states, often from colonial roots, that combine structures, methods, and interactions with the public in complex patterns that have become institutionalized and thus resistant to change. They provide order and predictability both for government personnel who have learned to work these patterns and for the public who have learned to adjust to them. There is some governmentwide integration in these patterns, enforced by standard legal, financial, accounting, procurement, and personnel regulations with which all government agencies must formally comply and that provide some elements of control for central government elites. In the operating agencies of government, however, in the various departments and public corporations, and especially in their field offices, there are usually elements of considerable flexibility that central controls do not fully reach. Such controls are interpreted away or effectively circumvented; political pressures and distinctive tasks create management problems that must be addressed expediently at the level of the individual program or service, often by officials on the ground. Despite central controls, officials in the pluralistic universe of government-sponsored activities confront distinctive management environments and problems. They can usually carve out space for operating autonomy and managerial discretion.

The tensions between central controls and operating discretion confront foreign and domestic reformers when they undertake management improvement. Normally reform efforts begin with a single activity—road maintenance, tax collection, agricultural extension, vocational education—and with specific changes in structure, staffing, procedures, or interaction with the public. Although many improvements can be implemented at this level, some may be blocked by standard rules, policies, or practices enforced by their ministries; despite heroic efforts at interpretation and evasion, needed changes cannot be applied at the agency or program level unless the ministry can be persuaded to alter its rules or practices. These changes may be technically possible if the internal politics of the ministry allows them, for example, if the medical doctors who control the ministry of health are willing to experiment with the provision of some health services at the community level by paraprofessionals. Ministry officials may be willing to modify their rules to allow reforms; often, however, they will protest that their hands are tied by rigid governmentwide rules relating, for example, to expenditure control, staff compensation, or contracting procedures. By this process, requests from operating levels for management improvement are escalated to the unpromising realm of governmentwide rules and practices, where the burden of proof is always on those who advocate changes, and reforms come slowly and painfully.

A prominent strategy for coping with this frustration—one that has been promoted by international development assistance agencies—has been to seek exemption for particular activities sponsored by foreign aid from standard government rules and practices, especially those relating to financial controls, personnel selection and compensation, procurement, and reporting. Although this enables short-term flexibility, it invariably generates resentment from agencies that are denied such autonomy. Such preferential treatment and freedom of action seldom survive the departure of the external donor; standard controls are gradually, often brutally, reimposed. The proliferation of semiautonomous agencies sharing responsibilities and even competing with those that operate according to standard administrative rules creates an unhealthy, even chaotic, environment in government. After the exemption strategy has lost its credibility, attention is likely to refocus on the substance and effects of the standard rules and practices, where changes are resisted in part because existing practices are widely known and produce predictable results, in part because the power of some officials depends on their ability to manipulate familiar management procedures. Incremental improvements are possible, however, if a convincing case can be reinforced by bureaucratic or political authority.

Many efforts at comprehensive governmentwide management reforms, especially of personnel, financial, or organizational systems, have been promoted by donor agencies. Most of them have employed top-down strategies, attempting to introduce and install structural or procedural changes such as performance budgeting, management by objectives, position classification, or management development schemes that had proved to be more or less successful in government or industry, touted as modern reforms, and propagated by schools of management in industrialized countries and by their clones in the Third World. The expectation has been that these modern, powerful technologies initiated at the top would permeate, invigorate, and leverage beneficial changes throughout the administrative system. Less developed countries (LDCs), alas, are littered with the debris of such aborted transplants, which threaten existing practices while failing to mobilize local support or respond to local demand. Such system-wide reforms appear to be too disruptive to familiar routines, and they threaten established power centers without being able to demonstrate convincingly the greater efficiency, effectiveness, financial savings, or probity that their advocates promise. Yet, in defiance of a history of failure, some donors, such as the United Nations Development Program's (UNDP's) recent Management Development Program, continue to promote the strategy of comprehensive, system-wide management development and reform.

The more successful efforts at management reform and improvement focus at the level of individual programs or organizations and build incrementally on familiar structures and procedures. They add features such as training, new technologies such as microcomputers, and opportunities for staff participation that are nonthreatening, confidence building, and rewarding. Reforms that shift the power balance—for example, decentralization of expenditure control or performance contracts for public enterprises—are more effective when they respond to specific government priorities that promise support from senior officials or respond to needs and demands from program operations rather than the systemwide wisdom of management specialists, foreign or domestic. Outdated systems involving, for example, procurement procedures, rigid-line item budgeting, or the frequent and apparently arbitrary transfer of management staff are more likely to yield to reforms prompted by their demonstrated costs to program operations, by organizational learning, and by incremental steps, than by top-down systems design. When systemwide reforms are attempted, they tend to break down in the face of passive resistance by staff who feel threatened or unpersuaded of their utility, while reformers and their sympathizers lack the power and the stamina to sustain their implementation.

The opposite approach is much more likely to yield lasting results. During the 1980s, in donor circles, structural adjustment— cutting back the role of the state in the economy through privatization, deregulation, and marketization—was "the only game in town." Donor agencies soon discovered that economic policy changes could not be self-executing. They depended on institutional reforms, management changes, and capacity development among ill-equipped and often reluctant government agencies, such as statistical offices, customs bureaus, central banks, and budget units. The new public-sector management units of the World Bank concentrated on this very small set of government operations, a tiny fraction of all the management-intensive activities of government, because these were deemed to be critical to the World Bank's high-priority economic policy objectives. They avoided the temptation to become embroiled in governmentwide systems, such as civil service or financial management, even though problems with these systems often complicated their reform objectives. Consistent with the program- and agency-specific approach outlined in this section, they wisely limited the scope of management improvement efforts to discrete activities. It was, however, a top-down process of reform activated not even by senior government officials but by an external donor agency, insisting on reforms as a condition for desperately needed financial assistance.

A bottom-up strategy of management reform, by contrast, begins with the identification of troubles or deficiencies at the point of service delivery or enforcement of regulations. It asks what substantive and management changes could contribute to more cost-effective and convenient performance, given political realities and unavoidable resource constraints, and taking full account of the advantages of coprovision and the interactive effects of service networks. Changes that can be introduced at the operating level should be, recognizing, however, that such reform ought to be treated as action hypotheses that will have to be adjusted and perhaps even abandoned in response to experience and organizational learning. Other proposals may have to be dealt with at higher levels in the management hierarchy where, in the face of pressures from below, some can be innovated, usually incrementally, aided by knowledge among senior managers of ideas and methods that have worked elsewhere. A few may require reforms in governmentwide systems. There too, incremental changes in response to specific government priorities or to demand from below are more likely to be successfully implemented than comprehensive reforms. At this level especially, experience from outside can be brought to bear by indigenous or foreign management specialists. This is an argument for demand-induced management changes and a strong caution against attempts at comprehensive reforms in governmentwide systems.

A certain iteration is possible between incremental demand-driven management improvements and systemwide reforms. The latter are likely to require (1) a widely perceived impression among attentive publics of breakdowns that cannot be accommodated by incremental changes, an impression that is shared by some influential insiders; and (2) senior politicians who are prepared to sponsor and commit some of their political capital to systemwide reforms often on faith and in response to the urging of foreign donors. With fortuitous timing, pressures from below may coincide with top-down initiatives to reform personnel, financial, procurement, organizational, or informational systems. Top-down management reforms, however, in the absence of some demand from within the ranks, are likely to fail, since they must be carefully adapted to local conditions and experience and integrated into ongoing processes. In the absence of a clear priority enunciated by senior officials and supported by demand from within the system derived from problems of performance, the presumption should run strongly against systemwide efforts at management reform. The strategy should instead start with recognition of specific deficiencies in performance. When incremental improvements prove insufficient, demand from below can build up to the point that more far-reaching changes seem needed and can mobilize a constituency among senior officials and the public. Despite the threats they imply and the learning and unlearning they usually entail, systemwide reforms then respond to and reinforce internal demand.

Initial interventions for management improvement should normally be at the point of service delivery or enforcement of regulations. This requires a more patient strategy of reform than has characterized so many attempts in the past, where leaders of Third World governments have been encouraged by foreign experts to believe that sweeping top-down reforms could dramatically transform and modernize management structures and managerial behavior—that the installation of new technologies would "streamline" the administrative system. But administrative performance is a human, not a mechanical, phenomenon; changes in human behavior tend to be incremental and require learning and the minimization of threat. These behavioral realities apply to senior as well as rank-and-file managers, all of whom have an impressive capacity for passive resistance to changes they consider unnecessary, infeasible, or damaging to their legitimate interests. Failure in performance is the most convincing evidence of necessity, incremental learning the most persuasive test of feasibility, and consultation, through participatory management, the best assurance that legitimate interests are being taken into account.

The preferred strategy for management reform should begin with the recognition of deficiencies in the performance of specific activities. When possible, reforms and improvements should be specific to the agency's problems and mission; the method should be incremental to ensure acceptance among those who must implement the reforms. Instead of comprehensive, systemwide reforms, management improvement normally depends on continuing incremental steps. Demand for broader governmentwide reforms should spring from unsatisfied needs within operating agencies and programs. A stream of demand-driven incremental management improvements can, in the Marxian sense, succeed in transforming quantity into quality.

INDIGENOUS METHODS

Modern management science has its roots in Western, especially Anglo-American, experience with large and complex organizations in the military, industrial, and governmental spheres. These societies attach high value to individual responsibility and individual achievement and to material incentives and rewards calibrated to performance, and they place a high value on the rigid scheduling of time (Moris 1981). They downplay the utility of nonmaterial incentives and the virtues of social solidarity as premises for management practices. Those who constructed this body of knowledge and the social technologies associated with it were confident not only that these were conducive to the rational and efficient use of resources and the accomplishment of collective goals, but also that they were universal in their applicability (Foster 1973). First through colonial penetration, and then since World War II on a much wider scale through foreign aid and economic expansion, Western management theory and practices have been widely diffused and adopted in LDCs. Schools of public administration and of business management have been important vehicles for the extension of Western management doctrine and practices, abetted often by zealous products of U.S. graduate education returning to their countries to apply this knowledge. But how universally applicable are Western management practices? Can they be the exclusive base for the science and practice of development management?

Technological development over the past two centuries has been mainly a Western—European and North American—phenomenon. It has incorporated powerful physical technologies, often based in the natural and physical sciences and embodied in vast arrays of machinery; cumulatively, these have transformed the human condition. They are conventionally denoted as hardware. Associated with the production and use of hardware are the social technologies or software, the methods of manipulating information and of directing human effort. Many of these are identified with modern management. Western-derived hardware has spread throughout the world, much of it now produced with few modifications in Third World countries. But is all Western-derived software, including management methods, equally suitable for non-Western countries (Moris 1976)? For many years it was assumed that Western management methods, like Western machinery, were as universally applicable as they were superior and more powerful because they embodied instrumental rationality. As recently as the late 1960s, some U.S. commentators referred to the "management gap" that seemed to threaten not only Third World but even European producers who aspired to compete with the United States.

Then came the non-Western Japanese. In a twenty-year surge beginning in about 1960, they became the world's most productive, efficient, and innovative economy, displacing the United States. Their industries built on advanced Western physical technologies, improved on them, then innovated both processes and products on their own. But their core management methods did not derive from Western concepts, practices, or experience. Though they borrowed extensively when they found it suitable, Japanese industry and government relied on home-grown management methods drawn from indigenous values and local experience. Well after these methods had demonstrated their efficacy and were being examined by Westerners for possible transfer and application, some Japanese scholars continued to dismiss these successful practices as outdated and "feudalistic" because they failed to conform to the canons of modernization, to standard, prestigious Western models and methods.

Management philosophy and methods are but one element of Japanese economic dynamism. But this should come as no surprise. Management is a set of social technologies. What works best in any society should reflect its dominant values and familiar practices, those that best motivate and sanction desired behavior among individuals and groups. As such values and behaviors are culturally conditioned and culturally distinctive, so also should be the management methods to which people respond. Some management methods may, of course, be transferred cross-culturally, as many Western technologies have been adapted in Japan and Japanese methods are now employed in automobile and electronics plants in North America. Cultures change.

Japanese experience is exemplary for other non-Western societies. All of them have some experience in conducting their affairs according to indigenous management norms and practices. Some indigenous practices have been displaced by contact with the West, but others survive. Incorporating indigenous values and experience, they continue to motivate behavior in ways that achieve acceptable results. Some no doubt cater to values other than instrumental efficiency or democratic fairness, but they yield predictable performance at acceptable levels of efficiency. My hypothesis—and it is only that at this stage—is that indigenous management methods are, *for some purposes,* more effective in motivating and guiding desired behavior than transplanted Western practices; and where they are deficient for some purposes, it may be possible to modify and improve them. There appears to be a disjunction between the imported management methods used with limited effectiveness in Third World governments and indigenous methods used successfully in local enterprises. Many of the latter are being used informally today in government agencies, often sub rosa, as they are not included in Western-inspired administrative manuals or in training curricula.

Effective as they are, they retain the stigma of backwardness. It is interesting to note that highly successful business firms operated by overseas Chinese in Southeast Asia and by Indians in East Africa have little contact with Western-oriented management training centers in these countries, and little is known about their management methods. The conventional explanation is that since these are mainly small family enterprises where relationships are based on trust, their management practices are not relevant or transferable to more formal organizations. These assertions should be subjected to critical scrutiny. The task of identifying, analyzing, and legitimatizing indigenous management technologies and their underlying philosophies and of adapting them to government operations should be taken up by the faculties and research staffs of the numerous schools and institutes of administration and management that now flourish throughout the Third World.

This is no call for the rejection of Western management knowledge or technologies, but it cautions against mindless imitation. It does, however, remind the reader that there are indigenous management experiences and methods, many of which are in fact practiced in organizations, including government agencies, that purport formally to be governed by Western rational processes. These bodies of practice remain largely neglected by scholars because they do not fit the dominant Western tradition. Some of these practices, such as those that depend on kinship loyalty, are inappropriate for government. Others such as Japanese doctrine and practices, which seemed to be an embarrassment to "modern" Japanese scholars, may prove to be valuable resources that can tap indigenous sources of motivation and legitimacy and thereby contribute to the management of social and economic development in their countries. They can also add to cross-cultural knowledge of the subject of development management.

THE ENIGMA OF POLITICS

The reality of politics continues to trouble students of management exactly as it does students of economics. Both of these disciplines are essentially technocratic in their outlook, seeking to maximize the rational and efficient use of resources in the production and distribution of goods and services. For both of them, politics gets in the way: politics as the expression of individual and group self-interest, politics as the competition for and exercise of power, politics as the adjustment of conflicts by compromises that distort and constrain the optimality of economic logic and of managerial rationality. Most government managers believe that politics should be confined to enacting laws, establishing policies, and approving budgets—the legitimate domain of politicians—but that implementation should be left to professional managers in a logical and sensible division of labor. But politicians, perversely, insist on encroaching on the managerial role; instead of protecting managers from political interference, all too often they exert their power to connive in such interference, weighing in on individual decisions and allocations, undermining the integrity of administration. Thus politics becomes a wild card, an unavoidable, unpredictable, unsavory, and corrupting reality. To some managers, politics is the main enemy, challenging the professional values to which they are committed—the rule of law, the pursuit of efficiency, objectivity, and equity. There is a noticeable tendency for career officials to feel more comfortable under military regimes that stifle political expression in society than under more open systems that confront them with political pressures. Yet they recognize that under most circumstances, managers must find ways to accommodate to political forces in order to survive.

Academic students of public administration who are rooted in the discipline of political science have less difficulty with politics. They see their task as describing, analyzing, and explaining the influence and effects of politics—of competing interests, of the uses of power—on administrative behavior and outcomes (Lapalombara 1963). Many of them accept politics as part of the context of all organized action in industry and voluntary associations as well as in government. They reject the conventional distinction between "policy" and "implementation," since action in pursuit of policy distributes benefits and costs unevenly among those with competitive stakes in the outcome. Thus calculations, choices, and consequences involving managers in the process of implementation are not merely instrumental, but political. They judge politics to be essentially beneficial, allowing legitimate, competitive societal interests, needs, grievances, and aspirations to be expressed, to find a place on the agendas of managers and government elites, to help shape and implement public policies, programs, and even specific allocations. They regard the interplay of group interests and their impacts on management as more important and more benign, if a choice must be made, than the technocratic achievement of instrumental rationality. With abuses of political power, with nepotism and corruption, they have more difficulty, noting, however, that more open politics may help to control these abuses and that managers are no less prone than politicians to indulge in such practices. The contribution of academic political scientists tends, however, to be detached and analytical, seldom prescriptive. To practitioners coping with politics and seeking guidance, they provide little help.

To those whose focus is less behavioral and more concerned with managerial achievement, politics is likely to be seen as less benign and much more threatening. To such scholars and managers, politics is less a means of clarifying objectives and affording publics the opportunity to influence the content and outputs of government activity than the distortion of rational program goals, the waste of resources, and the crude abuse of power. Thus managers aspire to keep politics at arm's length, defending themselves by rigid rules and procedures, referring requests for exceptions to hierarchical superiors, while recognizing that at times they must accommodate and even play the distasteful game themselves, bargaining with politicians and interest groups, adjusting their programs as far as their discretion allows, to exigent political demands.

The managerial mind, that model of man, is apolitical, often antipolitical. This set of attitudes is shaped and reinforced by professional education and training, which tend to emphasize technocratic logic. But politics is a reality that practicing development managers cannot escape, which indeed they must learn to embrace. Since there is a disjunction between management training, which is apolitical, and the realities that managers encounter on the job, political skills, understandings, and strategies tend to be self-taught. At the present state of the art, even the most sophisticated education in policy analysis can at best sensitize prospective managers to the political dimension of their roles, to the need to incorporate political variables into managerial calculations and choices, but it cannot teach reliable rules of engagement. In their political tasks, which become more important and consume a larger proportion of their time and energies as they advance in their careers, development managers are practicing an art that they learn mostly by experience. Such aphorisms as emerge from academic case studies are highly contingent; because of the number of variables involved, real-life managerial decisions that are implicated in political choices and political behavior are always judgmental.

It is easy for development managers to become cynical in the face of political forces from within government, including their own agencies, and from society that distort and even overwhelm what they consider to be the rational, efficient, and equitable execution of programs for which they are responsible. They may be compelled to award contracts to other than the most qualified bidder, to turn a blind eye to violators of regulations by politically connected individuals, to divert services from legally qualified to politically determined beneficiaries. They may be confronted with the choice between acquiescence in unsavory political decisions and the destruction of their careers. Persistent and aggressive political intervention may demoralize managers, undermine their commitment to program performance, and result in cynicism that degenerates into self-regarding careerism or even official corruption (Kohli 1990).

Successful development managers, however, find ways of converting necessity to opportunity. The risks that politics imposes cannot be eliminated, but they can be contained by recourse to law or by prudent accommodation. Managers learn how to exchange small favors for support that ensures and even enhances their access to needed resources and may incidentally even promote their own careers. They learn how to cultivate constituencies that can be relied upon to defend and promote their programs, but without paying too high a price. They learn the arts of bargaining and compromising that keep service networks functioning, trading off some efficiency for feasibility in a less than ideal world where politics is part of the natural order that can disturb and even undermine, but in the hands of skillful and committed practitioners, can also promote social and economic development. But if managers are looking beyond common sense and experience for practical guidance from academics who specialize in development management on how to handle the political dimensions of their professional roles, they cannot find it in any existing body of knowledge. At the current state of the art, they are mostly on their own.

MANAGERIAL PROFESSIONALISM
AND ITS ETHICAL DIMENSIONS

What motivates educated young men and women to choose careers in the civil service, careers as development managers? The denizens of neoclassical economics and of public choice theory are committed to a simple, straightforward, deductive psychological proposition: that men and women are—and indeed should be—motivated primarily by individual self-interest. Their goal is—and should be—the maximization of their personal power, prestige, income, wealth, and security; that goal is restrained only by the competitive self-interest of others and by fear of punishment for the violation of law. From this self-interested drive, not only the individual but all of society are presumed eventually to benefit as the fittest survive and prosper. As persons respond primarily to incentives for personal gain, government as well as industry should provide clear material incentives and rewards to evoke the desired individual effort and performance. There are many subtle variations of the rational individual self-interest theme, including some purporting to demonstrate that individual self-interest is often more rationally served by restraining its immediate fulfillment and respecting the needs and interests of others, in anticipation of reciprocity (Frank 1988). But the point of departure and the test of performance are still individual, mainly material self-interest.

The main alternative to the deformed moral universe of individual competitive greed situates the individual in social networks that generate solidarity, reciprocity, and mutual responsibility. Families, communities, associations, corporations of many kinds, and nations provide emotional security as well as economic satisfactions to individuals, in return for which individuals are expected to and indeed willingly fulfill numerous obligations to these collectivities and their members. They do not in every act calculate the net benefit to themselves. These obligations may extend not only to the present, but also to the future; the expectation is that persons should so behave today as to ensure the future security and welfare of the collectivity, its natural heritage, its physical environment, its culture, and its social institutions. The balancing of these entitlements and obligations applies with special force to persons in elite roles, including economic actors and government officials, extending their zone of solidarity from kinship and neighborhood to more inclusive collectivities. Civil servants, especially those in senior ranks, the managers, are expected to serve these broader collectivities—state and society—motivated primarily by duty and obligation, counterparts to the power and prestige as well as the salaries conferred on them by their managerial positions. The accent is less on individual self-interest and more on social responsibility.

Modern psychology has demonstrated that human behavior is actuated by mixed motives, not entirely by selfishness, not entirely by altruism, but by complex combinations that are hard to unravel and that vary with individuals, their socialization, their circumstances, and the cultures in which they function. Most individuals, including senior public managers, are not inclined to be saints or martyrs. They expect to be compensated fairly for their exertions and responsibilities, and they are in varying measures ambitious for advancement, recognition, material comfort, and security for themselves and their families. Although some are notably venal and self-serving, most attempt to reconcile their individual interests with their social and institutional responsibilities. The vulgar caricature of senior civil servants, as motivated primarily by cynical self-interest and responsive mainly to pecuniary and similar material incentives, is disproved by repeated observation in Third World states as well as in the most successful governments of industrialized societies. Although not unconcerned with their own careers, government managers commonly demonstrate a commitment to public values and to societal interests that compares more than favorably with that of the economic and political elites with whom they interact.

Impulses to serve the common interest may stem from respect for law, social solidarity, concern for the disadvantaged, duty, honor, or rectitude—desire to do the right thing. Jane Mansbridge (1990) quotes James Buchanan, who was awarded a Nobel Prize for applying the principles of neoclassical economics to political behavior, as conceding that bureaucrats may act not only in pursuit of selfish pecuniary interests, but "also [in pursuit] of what they genuinely consider to be the 'general interest' . . . the constraints, rules, and institutions within which persons make choices politically can and do influence the relative importance of the separate motivational elements" (p. 21). Buchanan is exactly right, but at the cost of abandoning the fundamental premise underlying the motivational structure of the "rational choice" model.

Commitment to the public interest is a function of the institutional role of government managers and of the ethos of public service that this role entails. There is a process of self-selection that makes government service particularly attractive to men and women already predisposed to the values of social responsibility. Professional education in public management socializes them into a set of expectations about appropriate behavior. The more professional the senior managers, the more likely they are to absorb, defend, and act out norms of official duty and social responsibility, and the better prepared they are to resist descent into cynicism when, as often happens, they are confronted with unethical blandishments or compelled to accept unpalatable compromises. In addition to professional education and socialization, the ethos enunciated and exemplified by political leadership also shapes the orientation and expectations of civil servants. The public service ethos proclaimed in the U.S. government during the Roosevelt and Kennedy years provided quite a different set of signals and incentives from that of the Reagan leadership, which celebrated the naked pursuit of individual material self-interest, limited only by the most literal legal constraints. Management, like politics, is the art of the possible, where the best may be the enemy of the attainable good, but what is believed to be possible depends greatly on the values that key actors bring to their managerial tasks.

Development managers are unavoidably endowed with discretion in their decisions and in their actions—decisions and actions that necessarily affect the allocation of resources, costs, and benefits among individuals and groups in the public. Their decisions also influence the effectiveness, efficiency, and responsiveness of government services and regulations. What they do is consequential. Their discretion conveys power that can be controlled and held accountable by external forces such as judicial and auditing restraints, bureaucratic and political superiors, societal interest groups, and the diffuse effects of political culture. They can also be controlled by internal self-discipline, reinforced by a public-service ethos (Weber 1947). External sources of control, especially in LDCs, tend to function sporadically and with uncertain effects. The claims of political elites and of societal interest groups may sometimes be so self-serving that responsible development managers must be prepared to fend them off, hence the social utility of discretion in their hands. But this discretion is vulnerable to abuse unless it is controlled and guided by internalized professional values. Bureaucratic responsibility hinges on the self-discipline of its senior cadres, a self-discipline guided by their professional ethos. Development managers in the public sector are at the mercy of forces beyond their control unless they succeed in achieving professional status.

What are the dimensions of managerial professionalism in the framework of Third World development? There are three such dimensions. The first is the mastery of a body of knowledge and of operational skills obtained by specialized education and enriched by career experience. This body of knowledge combines management science with substantive competence in one or more sectors of development policy such as finance, agriculture, urban affairs, human services, or public works, so that managers are credibly equipped to participate in policy development and to supervise the implementation of substantively complex development programs. Government may recruit its development managers from many sources in order to achieve an appropriate distribution of substantive and operational competencies, but it must invest deliberately in in-service education, for example, in executive development programs, to ensure the continual upgrading of managerial skills and understandings and the reinforcement of their professional ethos.

The second dimension of managerial professionalism, institutional respect, follows from the first. Higher-level skills and competencies in substantive policy and managerial operations entitle these cadres to a measure of social respect. This implies that senior management positions normally should be filled by competitive performance from within the ranks of the government's management cadres. If such positions are frequently filled on patronage grounds by unqualified political loyalists, the professional status of the development management cadres cannot be sustained. This respect also implies that political decision makers will take account of the information and advice provided by career managers even when they decline to follow that advice; that knowledge of their status and competence reinforces the authority of career managers when dealing with influential members of the public from the private sector and associational groups, in shaping and applying public policy, and in the management of service networks. If it is to be sustained, institutional respect must be earned by performance.

The third dimension of managerial professionalism is the set of ethical norms into which candidate managers are socialized by their backgrounds, education, and experience. These ethical norms characterize their distinctive roles, and provide internalized guidance for their decisions and their actions. The importance of a conscious professional ethos is even more critical for Third World development managers than for their counterparts in industrialized countries; among the latter, their professional ethos tends to be reinforced by the prevailing political culture, while in LDCs this ethos may be at odds with important societal expectations about relationships between government and society. There are three main themes that ought to be included in the professional ethos of development managers.

Public Trust

The first is the concept of officeholding as a public trust, totally divorced from personal, kinship, or ethnic interests and in no event to be exploited for particularistic advantage. Allocations controlled by public office are, as far as possible, to be determined objectively by law and never by considerations of personal, partisan, or commercial advantage. Civil servants are to depend only on their salaries, modest though they may be, and never on rents or illegal side payments. When salaries no longer provide a minimum decent livlihood, as has occurred in several Third World governments, managers are forced to compromise their professional ethos in pursuit of alternative income or to sacrifice it by resorting to official corruption.

The rigid separation of official from personal interests and the notion of officials as trustees or stewards of public resources are crucial to the conduct of public affairs in which society can have confidence, despite unremitting pressures to divert government resources on a privileged or preferential basis to particular interests. Officeholders in developing countries are constantly subject to such pressures and temptations, this being the root of official corruption. The determination of officials to reject such pressures and public recognition that respect for law is indeed the governing norm is the key to confidence in public management and to the very legitimacy of government. The trusteeship notion, the separation of the official from the personal realm, is an uncompromising requirement of a professional management ethos.

Service to Society

The second theme commits development managers to an ethos of service, to the polity and to society—not the mechanical enforcement of regulations or the performance of routines, but the shaping of government policies and programs to respond to societal needs as fully, fairly, and objectively as possible. Because the means are always scarcer than legitimate claims on resources, and these claims are inherently competitive, development managers have the task of apportioning limited means in response to public demands in ways that enhance the productivity of these resources and their equitable distribution, values that at times may be in conflict. An ethos of service tempers the power and discretion that development managers enjoy and makes them mindful of the consequences of their actions. Service, consequences, results—these should be more important as guides to action than procedures and routines.

This theme relates to style as well as to substance. A service orientation, one that emphasizes results, can be patronizing to the public, preferring that they remain grateful but passive beneficiaries of government largesse. This posture is an easy temptation to members of a highly educated professional cadre, but it is both ethically inappropriate and functionally ineffective. It is ethically inappropriate because it implies a lack of respect for the lower-status members of the public whom the managers are committed to serve; ineffective because it fails to tap the knowledge, skills, experience, and enthusiasm that can inspire the coproduction and coprovision of services, enhance the effectiveness of government contributions, and activate the public in the direction of individual and collective self-reliance. The theme of service is essential, but it must be combined with another imperative: respect for and responsiveness to the members of society at whom their programs are directed. This respect and responsiveness must include the distinctive needs and contributions of women to the development of their societies—a potential that development managers can no longer afford to neglect.

Protection for the Disadvantaged

The third of these ethical themes focuses the efforts and energies of development managers not only on service, but more specifically on developmental goals, especially those that enhance the productivity, security, quality of life, and efficacy of the weaker and less advantaged sectors of society (Chambers 1983). In LDCs, the disadvantaged are demographically a substantial proportion of society, often a majority. The service theme is important, in that it sensitizes development managers to the consequences of their actions. But a special claim on their attention and on the resources they control should, when there is a reasonable choice, be those in greatest need. Vigorous economic growth is essential to broadly based development, but it is never sufficient to ensure fair distribution. Many growth strategies, including donor interventions, inadvertently increase poverty in the short run (Adelman and Morris 1973). This is also true of structural adjustment programs. Protecting the disadvantaged is a vital function of enlightened government and thus a responsibility of development managers. Policies and programs that channel productive opportunities to the majority of smallholders, landless laborers, microentrepreneurs, and urban workers in the nonformal sector and that cultivate the skills required to use them can facilitate extensive and sustained growth along with a broadly based distribution of benefits. Equity as well as growth should be incorporated into the value systems of professional development managers.

That this theme produces ethical dilemmas should not be surprising. The economically and socially weaker elements of society tend to be weak in political efficacy as well, in the ability to claim resources on behalf of their economic productivity and social well-being. Moreover, resources in the hands of those better equipped with capital and skills may, in the short run at least, make a greater contribution to aggregate economic growth and especially to the vital supply of foreign exchange. Especially in an era that celebrates free-market economics, an ethical concern for the disadvantaged may impose burdens and risks on development managers. They must faithfully implement laws and policies that may not be helpful to the disadvantaged, while employing what influence and discretion they command to channel resources and opportunities for the benefit of the poor. This dimension of their professional role requires both courage and skill, since it may force development managers to swim against powerful currents in their governments and often among influential donors to find ways to vindicate their ethical commitments but without destroying their careers.

Managerial professionalism in Third World development contexts requires cognitive knowledge and operating skills. But these must be disciplined and guided by an ethos that emphasizes integrity, service, and commitment to development goals. Because of this indispensable ethical component, development management is not merely a vocation that earns a livelihood along with some prestige and power. Beyond that, it is a calling that combines opportunities for great personal satisfaction with heavy responsibilities. A mere decade ago, in most academic circles, confronting the ethical dimensions of administration and management would have appeared impractical and awkward, a proper concern for moralists but certainly not for scientists. Today it is accepted that values, conscious or not, are inherent in all human action and especially relevant to public administration (Cooper 1990; Richter, Burke, and Doig 1990; Bowman 1991). Development management is explicitly committed to improving the lot of Third World peoples under conditions of uncertainty where mistakes, failures, and institutionalized abuse are continuing realities. An explicitly ethical orientation is not only appropriate, it is the very foundation of development management as a profession.

MANAGEMENT EDUCATION AND TRAINING

The cultivation and practice of management capacities cannot be confined to the state and large business firms. Management potential is widely diffused in any population. Under a pluralistic strategy of development, it is important that government provide facilities for the development and enhancement of latent management capabilities among small enterprises, voluntary associations, and local authorities. Society is likely to yield very high returns for modest investments and expenditures committed to the cultivation of this critical category of human resources. One of the responsibilities of public-sector development managers is to strengthen, expand, and protect wherever possible the centers that provide broad-based opportunities for the leaders and managers of organizations outside the circles of government.

In this section, however, I focus on professional education and training for public-sector managers because their role is so catalytic to social and economic development. Frequent references have been made to this subject in previous chapters, especially in Chapter 5. Here I expand on their implications for professional performance and on the content of career-oriented management training. The insights, attitudes, and skills that equip public development managers for their responsibilities come from many sources that are independent of formal education or training. These range from the personality endowments of individuals to their general educational preparation and the values and behaviors that are fostered by the cultures into which they are socialized. They include experiences on the job, the policy frameworks in which managers function, and the motivational effects of material and nonmaterial incentives and sanctions. Because of the multiple influences that determine managerial behavior, it is sometimes argued that while administration and management can be learned mainly by experience, they do not constitute a body of knowledge or practices that can be taught.

This counsel, however, has not persuaded governments of LDCs or donor agencies (Paul 1983; Kerrigan and Luke 1987; Swerdlow and Ingle 1974).

Even conceding some reservations about the utility of formal education and training for management roles, there remains an underlying confidence that disciplined knowledge can make significant differences in managerial behavior and management performance, that such knowledge can be imparted systematically and learned, that the potential benefits greatly exceed the modest expenditures of money and staff time, and that these expenditures constitute investments in human resources that are vital to the performance of governments. Schools and institutes devoted to management education and training, as well as to research and consultative services, have consequently proliferated in LDCs. A decade ago, the number of institutions devoted to public administration training totaled 276 in 91 LDCs (International Association of Schools and Institutes of Public Administration 1981). In addition to these centers that focus on general public management, there are numerous government-sponsored facilities that include management as a component of training for individual sectors or programs.

The quality of the education and training that these centers provide has been found to be variable; although there are instances of considerable sophistication and emphasis on developmental activities, much of the formal training has been limited in scope, focused mainly on management technologies and routines, and unresponsive to the needs of senior development managers. The management needs of voluntary associations and of local authorities tend to be neglected. Though specialized educational and training facilities exist for private enterprise, their curricula tend to be modeled after Western business schools that overlook the weight of government in the business environment of LDCs.

For public development managers, there are three principal levels of instruction: the preentry university level; the mid-career level for serving officers, including the transition of subject matter specialists to management responsibilities; and the executive development level for senior management staff. The emphasis in content and in learning processes must necessarily accommodate the different experiences and responsibilities of officers at each level. Preentry instruction requires a large didactic component; the learning environment for senior staff should be informal, loosely structured, and provide for the participation of senior counterparts from business firms, voluntary associations, local authorities, and key politicians. The proportion of curricula that focus on development-related problems rather than on managerial routines should increase at every level, especially for senior officials. If the assessment in this book of the roles of professional development managers in the framework of pluralistic strategies is at all valid, then their education and training ought to include the following components:

1. For the *instrumental* functions of management, emphasis on:
   - Generic management technologies—financial, personnel and human relations, informational, supervisory, structural, procedural—which continue to comprise the bread-and-butter responsibilities of managers in public bureaucracies.
   - Program management—the processes of design, implementation, and evaluation of individual service, regulatory, enterprise, and promotional activities sponsored by governments.

2. For the *political* functions:
   - Skills of policy analysis, both generic and as they apply to the substantive sectors in which managers are expected to achieve specialized competence.
   - Sensitivity to methods for coping with interbureaucratic influences, societal forces, and political interventions that impinge on program operations.
   - Appreciation of the differential benefits and costs of policy and program outputs on the publics that they affect.

3. For the *entrepreneurial* function, the opportunities and limitations of proactive management styles outside normal operating routines, including managerial interventions that attempt to modify policies, invigorate operations, recombine resources in fresh patterns, and enhance both staff and public participation in program operations.

4. For the *interorganizational* function, analytical insights, such as linkage management, and operating skills, such as environmental mapping, required for policy and program implementation that involve two or more government agencies and especially the multi-institutional service networks discussed in Chapter 6.

5. For the *public interest* function:
   - Skills in identifying and articulating long-term societal goals and in shaping policies and programs that implement these goals.
   - Criteria and methods of dealing with the ethical dilemmas that inevitably confront senior development managers.

For public development managers, I have identified five functions or roles, each requiring distinctive curriculum content, and three principal levels of instruction. The specifics of how curriculum content ought to be constructed and distributed over these levels of instruction cannot be prescribed for the variety of training centers in LDCs, given their differing structures and circumstances. All the functions would be addressed at each level but with different intensity. In general, I expect that the basic preentry level of education and training would focus on instrumental functions; the intermediate level would emphasize program management and entrepreneurial roles; the advanced level would concentrate on political and interorganizational responsibilities. All of them would be compelled to struggle with the ethical problems inherent in the public-interest function.

ACCOUNTABILITY AMID UNCERTAINTY
AND COMPLEXITY

The administration of development activities in Third World settings confronts managers with high levels of uncertainty and complexity. Uncertainty is the product of limited and often unreliable information about the natural and social environments in which development initiatives occur, as well as the acute shortages and the conflicts that produce instability and turbulence. Complexity is partly a function of societal heterogeneity, confronting managers with publics that have varying resources, needs, and expectations, and partly of structural diversity within and among more or less autonomous organizations whose activities must be coordinated in many cases through service networks. Uncertainty may be reduced by the collection and evaluation of baseline data at the initiation of development projects and by ongoing monitoring of both process and performance. Investment in more timely and accurate information can mitigate the problem of uncertainty, but can never overcome it. Conventional management attempts to protect itself from uncertainty by the imposition of rules and routines that produce some predictability by compelling society to adjust to the requirements of government, but at considerable cost to government's ability to respond to the priorities, convenience, and changing needs of its various publics.

Some writers continue to urge administrative simplicity as a prescription for program effectiveness (Israel 1987). But the simplicity that should be aimed for is more in the services that are provided than in the structures through which they are produced. Integrated rural development projects broke down in the 1970s because the number and diversity of the services involved overwhelmed the coordinating capacities of the governments (Montgomery 1983). Organizational complexity, however, is an inevitable reality in all large-scale enterprises, industrial as well as governmental, for reasons discussed in Chapter 4; this inherent complexity is compounded by the interorganizational necessities associated with development management, as outlined in Chapters 5 and 6. Instead of deploring structural complexity, development managers must be prepared to cope with it and indeed to embrace it, since it is an unavoidable consequence of pluralistic strategies of development. Uncertainty, on the other hand, can be reduced by greater attention to information as well as by processes of administrative decentralization and participatory management, which provide incentives for local problem-solving behavior.

The training of development managers should condition them to work in environments characterized by uncertainty and organizational complexity. They should expect to confront these realities as a normal part of their jobs, recognizing the limitations of rigorous planning and programming and accepting the inevitability of organizational learning, incremental adjustments, and judgmental decisions often under severe time pressures and inadequate information. Above all, they must learn that neither uncertainty nor complexity can be acceptable reasons for inaction and that career rewards accrue to those who are able to act effectively in the face of ambiguity and risk.

As development managers are not free agents, they face continuous tensions between responsiveness to their publics and accountability to hierarchical superiors. Their discretion is limited by law, by official policies, by personnel and especially financial regulations, by resource limitations, and by political exigencies. The constraints of bureaucratic discipline weigh heavily on most managers; under prevailing rules and incentives, their careers may be more at risk from the violation of formal rules than they would be advanced by innovative and responsive service to the public. Even under a regime of incentives designed to promote and reward responsiveness downward, accountability upward to political and bureaucratic superiors will continue to be a necessary and legitimate limitation on public managers' freedom of action. Not all societal demands deserve bureaucratic responsiveness; some self-interested claims for favorable treatment ought to be resisted and rejected. Resourceful managers oriented to responsiveness can often—but not always—find loopholes in the rules, which by astute interpretation enable them to reconcile the formalities of accountability upward with timely and adaptive service to particular publics. Although this process can expand managerial discretion, it does not displace the need for or the actual practice of accountability.

Service- and performance-oriented managers must be conscious of tensions between two legitimate competing claims on their loyalties, accountability to superiors and responsiveness to publics. They must attempt to satisfy them both, to reconcile these dual obligations and pressures. The common plea in the development administration literature for greater responsiveness is predicated on the need to relax the conventional bureaucratic tendencies and incentives to procedural rigidity, uniformity, standardization, and boundary maintenance enforced by heavy-handed accountability upward and allow for greater managerial discretion and initiative to accommodate public demand and local circumstances. Increased priority to responsiveness requires reforms in structures, procedures, and incentives such as those outlined in Chapter 3, reinforced by professional training and ethical commitments discussed earlier in this chapter.

The literature on development administration never contemplated the abandonment of financial, legal, or programmatic accountability upward or questioned its necessity, in the absence of which governments would lose control of the activities for which they are responsible and risk grave abuses and inequities. Balancing responsiveness downward with accountability upward, tilting where resourcefulness permits in the direction of responsiveness, coping with uncertainty, and embracing complexity are inescapable dimensions of the development management role in the framework of a pluralistic development strategy.

PERFORMANCE GOALS AND CRITERIA

This book has elaborated the basic concepts, summarized below:

1. Economic and social development cannot depend on the initiative and guidance of a handful of elites centered either in the state or in large capitalist firms. State-dominated development strategies have been at best insufficient and at worst dismal failures. Creative initiatives must, instead, be stimulated, activated, welcomed, and rewarded in all sectors of society, including profit-making market-based firms, voluntary and community associations, and local authorities. Under pluralistic strategies of development, the state retains responsibility for such critical functions as (a) establishing policy regimes that promote economic efficiency and expansion; (b) operating and maintaining the physical and social infrastructures of society; (c) enforcing regulations that protect public health and safety, the integrity of financial institutions, natural resources, and the environment; and (d) providing services that facilitate economic productivity and social well-being, including management education and training. The state should not, however, aspire to be a monopoly supplier of services. Many goods and services are and more ought to be coproduced and coprovided by agencies of government in association with private firms, local authorities, and voluntary associations.

2. A pluralistic strategy of development produces complex relationships—interorganizational within government, interinstitutional between government agencies and societal collectivities. These linkages generate the service networks that are increasingly responsible for many of the activities that take place outside individual households or firms and outside market exchanges. In many respects, the service networks are self-organizing, regulated by processes of mutual accom-

modation, but senior development managers from government retain an important role in shaping and maintaining them and in brokering the dynamic arrangements that satisfy participants in the networks while allowing their joint activities to proceed.

3. The activities of management are central to the development enterprise—in voluntary associations, local authorities, and private firms as well as government. Deficiencies in management have been associated with failures in development activities even when policies and politics are favorable. Managerial skills, insights, and sensitivities can be taught and learned; they can be evoked by regimes of incentives and rewards, including pressures from activated and demanding publics. Management in the public sector continues to focus on the operations of individual programs in single complex organizations. Increasingly, however, high-level management must cope with multiorganizational networks that include governmental as well as nongovernmental components, where hierarchical authority is displaced by entrepreneurial and political skills as the principal tools of development managers. Between the supervision of routines and the highly visible acts and pronouncements of politicians lie the anonymous development managers whose contingent and often risky judgments at the margins of management and politics directly affect the implementation of development activities. In the mixture of motives that drive performance among senior officials—security, ambition, duty, achievement orientation, ethical commitment—the latter must be specially cultivated to evoke the public-regarding and developmental values that alone justify the power that is invested in their role. The ethical dimension of development management both disciplines and ennobles their performance.

4. Specific goals pursued by senior development managers in government and the criteria by which their performance should be evaluated vary with individual programs, but they can be aggregated under five headings. The classical managerial goals of *effectiveness*, achieving intended outputs, and of *efficiency*, the economical employment of resources, remain necessary but not sufficient guides for development managers. Management performance must be oriented to and assessed by three additional and interrelated values: *outreach*, success in generating participation and resource contributions from society, as evidenced by patterns of coproduction and coprovision in service networks; *responsiveness*, success in catering to actual demand and to latent needs among relevant publics while respecting their preferences and convenience; and *sustainability*, success in ensuring the continuity of services by innovating and adapting to changing circumstances, maintaining

supportive constituencies, and recruiting the required resources. These are the exacting but attainable criteria by which development managers should expect to be judged.

5. The development enterprise in the final decade of this century is beset with daunting problems—explosive population growth; environmental degradation; grinding poverty and human suffering in urban as well as rural settlements; exploitation by greedy, self-regarding, corrupt, and all too often incompetent economic and political elites. In confronting these realities, pessimism becomes a brooding temptation that can paralyze the will, engendering cynicism and defeatism among domestic decision makers and foreign donors alike. The need to resist and transcend the descent into despair becomes a moral imperative, especially for senior politicians, development managers, and the scientists and academicians who provide them with essential intellectual support. That non-Westerners can achieve economic success has been conclusively demonstrated by the Japanese and Taiwanese; that recently poor societies can accomplish the transition to prosperity has been proved by the Koreans, Thais, and Malaysians; that some regions in lagging countries can prosper is evidenced in the Indian Punjab, the Sao Paulo conurbation of Brazil, and the Kenyan Highlands. An abiding confidence that, despite setbacks and negative short-term prospects, men and women remain capable of shaping their collective futures must be the essential article of faith for persons seriously participating in the development enterprise. In the face of harsh realities, this faith and confidence constitute the armor that enables development managers to sustain the instrumental activism that is critical to their professional mission.

REFERENCES

Adelman, I., and C. T. Morris (1973). *Economic Growth and Social Equity in Developing Countries*. Stanford, CA: Stanford University Press.

Aldrich, H. (1979). *Organizations and Environments*. Englewood Cliffs, NJ: Prentice Hall.

Amin, S. (1976). *Unequal Development*. New York: Monthly Review Press.

Appleby, P. (1945). *Big Government*. New York: Knopf.

Baaklani, A., and J. J. Heaphey, eds. (1977). *Comparative Legislative Reforms and Innovations*. Albany, NY: SUNY Graduate School of Public Affairs.

Bennett, A. (1990). Performance contracts and public enterprise performance. In *Public Enterprise*. See Heath (1990).

Bennis, W. (1969). *Organizational Development: Its Nature, Origins and Prospects*. Reading, MA: Addison-Wesley.

Blair, H. (1985). Reorienting development administration. *Journal of Development Studies* 21:449–57.

Blase, M. G. (1986). *Institution Building: A Sourcebook* (rev. ed.). Columbia, MO: University of Missouri Press.

Blau, P. M. (1963). *The Dynamics of Bureaucracy*. Chicago: University of Chicago Press.

Bossert, T. J., and D. A. Parker (1982). *The Politics and Administration of Primary Health Care: A Literature Review and Research Strategy*. Hanover, NH: Dartmouth College Department of Community and Family Medicine.

Bowman, J., ed. (1991). *Ethical Frontiers in Public Management: Seeking New Strategies for Resolving Ethical Dilemmas*. San Francisco: Jossey-Bass.

Bozeman, B. (1987). *All Organizations Are Public*. San Francisco: Jossey-Bass.

Braibanti, R. (1969). *Political and Administrative Development*. Durham, NC: Duke University Press.

Brinkerhoff, D. (1990). *Improving Development Program Performance: Guidelines for Managers*. Boulder, CO: Lynn Reinner Publishers.

Bryant, C., and L. G. White (1982). *Managing Development in the Third World*. Boulder, CO: Westview Press.

Caiden, N., and A. Wildavsky (1974). *Planning and Budgeting in Poor Countries.* New York: John Wiley and Sons.

Carroll, T. J., and J. D. Montgomery, eds. (1987). *Supporting Grassroots Organizations.* Cambridge, MA: Lincoln Institute of Land Management.

Chairman, Development Assistance Committee (1989). *Report: Development Cooperation in the 1990s: Efforts and Policies of the Members of the DAC.* Paris: Organization for Economic Cooperation and Development.

Chambers, R. (1974). *Managing Rural Development: Ideas and Experience from East Africa.* Uppsala: Scandinavian Institute of African Studies (reissued in 1985, West Hartford, CT: Kumarian Press).

———— (1983). *Rural Development: Putting the Last First.* London: Longmans.

Charlton, S. E. M., J. Everett, and K. Staudt, eds. (1989). *Women, the State, and Development.* Albany, NY: State University of New York Press.

Chaturvedi, A. (1988). *District Administration: The Dynamics of Discord.* New Delhi: Sage Publications.

Cheema, G. S., and D. Rondinelli (1983) *Decentralization and Development: Policy Implementation in Developing Countries.* Beverly Hills, CA: Sage Publications.

Churchman, G. W. (1968). *The Systems Approach.* New York: Delacorte Press.

Cohen, J. M., and N. Uphoff (1977). *Rural Development Participation: Concepts and Measures for Project Design, Implementation and Evaluation.* Ithaca, NY: Cornell University, Rural Development Committee.

Cooper, T. L. (1990). *The Responsible Administrator: An Approach to Ethics for the Administative Role* (3d ed.). San Francisco: Jossey-Bass.

Davis, S., and P. Lawrence (1977). *Matrix.* Reading, MA: Addison-Wesley.

Durkheim, E. (1933). *The Division of Labor in Society.* Glencoe, IL: Free Press.

Dutton, W., and K. Kraemer (1985). *Modeling as Negotiating: The Political Dynamics of Computer Models in the Policy Process.* Norwood, NJ: Ablex Publishing.

Dwyer, D., and J. Bruce, eds. (1988). *A House Divided: Women and Income in the Third World.* Stanford, CA: Stanford University Press.

Easton, D. (1965). *A Framework for Political Analysis.* Englewood Cliffs, NJ: Prentice Hall.

Eaton, J., ed. (1972). *Institution Building: From Concepts to Application.* Beverly Hills, CA: Sage Publications.

Economist (1990). "The State of the Nation-State." London. 22 Dec., pp. 43–47

Esman, M. J. (1966). The politics of development administration. In *Approaches to Development.* See Montgomery and Siffin (1966).

———— (1972 a). *Administration and Development in Malaysia: Institution Building and Reform in a Plural Society.* Ithaca, NY: Cornell University Press.

———— (1972 b). The elements of institution building. In *Institution Building.* See Eaton (1972).

———— (1983). *Paraprofessionals in Rural Development: Issues in Field Level Staffing for Agricultural Projects.* World Bank Staff Working Paper No. 573.

Esman, M. J., R. Colle, E. Taylor, and N. T. Uphoff (1980). *Paraprofesssionals in Rural Development.* Ithaca, NY: Cornell University, Rural Development Committee.

Esman, M. J., and J. D. Montgomery (1969). Systems approaches to technical cooperation: The role of development administration. *Public Administration Review* 29(5): 507–39.

Esman, M. J., and N. T. Uphoff (1984). *Local Organizations: Intermediaries in Rural Development*. Ithaca, NY: Cornell University Press.

Evans, P. V., D. Rueschemeyer, and T. Scocpol (1985). *Bringing the State Back in*. New York: Cambridge University Press.

Fainsod, M. (1963). The structure of development administration. In *Development Administration*. See Swerdlow (1963).

Ferris, J. M. (1984). Coprovision: Citizen time and money donations in public service provision. *Public Administration Review* 44(4): 324–33.

Foley, D. (1989). *Non-Governmental Organizations as Catalysts of Policy Reform and Social Change*. Ph.D. dissertation, University of Southern California.

Foster, G. (1973). *Traditional Societies and Technological Change*. New York: Harper & Row.

Frank, A. G. (1972). *Capitalism and Underdevelopment in Latin America*. New York: Monthly Review Press.

Frank, R. (1988). *Passion Without Reason: The Strategic Role of the Emotions*. New York: W. W. Norton.

Friedman, M. (1963). *Capitalism and Freedom*. Chicago: University of Chicage Press.

Gable, R. W., ed. (1959). *Partnership for Progress: International Technical Cooperation*. Philadelphia: American Academy of Political and Social Science.

Garcia-Zamor, J-C. (1977). *The Ecology of Development Administration in Jamaica, Trinidad, Tobago, and Barbados*. Washington, DC: Organization of America States.

Gerlach, L., and V. H. Hine (1970). *People, Power, and Change: Movements of Social Transformation*. Indianapolis: Bobbs-Merrill.

Goodsell, C. T. (1983). *The Case for Bureaucracy*. Chatham, NJ: Chatham House Publishers.

Gross, B. (1964). *The Management of Organizations*. New York: Free Press of Glencoe.

——— (1967). *Action Under Planning: The Guidance of Economic Development*. New York: McGraw Hill.

Gulick, L., and L. Urwick, eds. (1954). *Papers on the Science of Administration* (3d ed.). New York: Institute of Public Administration.

Hage, J., and K. Finsterbusch (1987). *Organizational Change as a Development Strategy: Models and Tactics for Improving Third World Organizations*. Boulder, CO: Lynne Reinner Publishers.

Hanf, K., and F. Scharpf (1978). *Interorganizational Policy Making: Limits to Coordination and Central Control*. London: Sage.

Hanf, K., and T. A. J. Toonen (1985). *Policy Implementation in Unitary and Federal Systems*. Dordrecht: Martinus Nijhoff Publishers.

Hanson, A. H. (1959). *Public Enterprise in Economic Development*. London: Routledge and Kegan Paul.

Hayek, F. A. (1990). *Economic Freedom*. Cambridge, MA: Basil Blackwell.

Heady, F. (1966). *Public Administration: A Comparative Perspective*. Englewood Cliffs, NJ: Prentice Hall.

Heady, F., and S. Stokes, eds. (1962). *Papers in Comparative Public Administration*. Ann Arbor, MI: University of Michigan, Institute of Public Administration.

Heath, J. (1990). *Public Enterprise at the Crossroads*. London: Routledge.

Higgins, B. (1959). *Economic Development: Principles, Policies, and Problems*. New York: W. W. Norton.

Hirschmann, D. (1981). Development or underdevelopment administration? A further deadlock. In *Development and Change* (vol. 12). Beverly Hills, CA: Sage Publications.

Holdcroft, L. (1978). *The Rise and Fall of Community Development in Developing Countries.* Michigan State University, Rural Development Paper No. 2.

Honadle, G. H., and J. VanSant (1986). *Implementation for Sustainability.* West Hartford, CT: Kumarian Press.

Horowitz, D. (1985). *Ethnic Groups in Conflict.* Berkeley, CA: University of California Press .

Hult, K., and C. W. Walcott (1990). *Governing Public Organizations: Politics, Structures and Institutional Design.* Pacific Grove, CA: Brooks-Cole Publishing Co.

Inayatullah, M., ed. (1976). *Management Training for Development: The Asian Experience.* Kuala Lumpur: Asian Center for Development Administration.

————, ed. (1979). *Approaches to Rural Development: Some Asian Experiences.* Kuala Lumpur: Asian and Pacific Development Administration Center.

Ingle, M. (1979). *Implementing Development Programs: A State of the Art Review.* Syracuse, NY: Syracuse University Press.

International Association of Schools and Institutes of Public Administration (1981). *Directory.* Washington, DC: Author.

Israel, A. (1987). *Institutional Development: Incentives and Performance.* Baltimore, MD: Johns Hopkins University Press.

Jantsch, E. (1980). *The Self-Organizing Universe.* Oxford, England: Pergamon Press.

Jones, L. P., and R. Moran (1982). *Public Enterprise in Less Developed Countries.* Cambridge, England: Cambridge University Press.

Katz, D., and R. L. Kahn (1978). *The Social Psychology of Organizations.* New York: John Wiley and Sons.

Katz, S. M. (1970). Exploring a systems approach to development administration. In *Frontiers of Development Administration.* See Riggs (1971).

Kerrigan, J., and J. S. Luke (1987). *Management Training Strategies for Developing Countries.* Boulder, CO: Lynne Reinner Publishers.

Keynes, J. M. (1936). *The General Theory of Employment, Interest, and Money.* New York: Harcourt Brace.

Kiggundu, M. N. (1989). *Managing Organizations in Developing Countries: An Operational and Strategic Approach.* West Hartford, CT: Kumarian Press.

Klitgaard, R. (1989). Incentive myopia. *World Development* 17(4):447–59.

Kohli, A. (1990). *Democracy and Disorder: India's Growing Crisis of Governability.* New York: Cambridge University Press.

Korten, D. (1980). Community organization and rural development. *Public Administration Review* 40:480–511.

Korten, D., and R. Klauss (1984). *People-Centered Development: Contributions Toward Theory and Planning Frameworks.* West Hartford, CT: Kumarian Press.

Kotler, P. (1976). *Marketing Management: Analysis, Planning and Control.* Englewood Cliffs, NJ: Prentice Hall.

Lapalombara, J. (1963). *Bureaucracy and Political Development.* Princeton, NJ: Princeton University Press.

Laudon, K. (1974). *Computers and Bureaucratic Reform: The Political Function of Urban Information Systems*. New York: John Wiley and Sons.

Lawler, E. E. (1983). *Design of Effective Reward Systems*. Los Angeles: University of Southern California, Graduate School of Business.

———— (1988). *High Involvement Management*. San Francisco: Jossey-Bass.

Leonard, D. K. (1977). *Reaching the Peasant Farmer: Organization Theory and Practice in Kenya*. Chicago: University of Chicago Press.

Leonard, D. K., and D. R. Marshall, eds. (1982). *Institutions of Rural Development for the Poor: Decentralization and Organizational Linkages*. Berkeley, CA: University of California Institute of International Studies.

Lewis, W. A. (1955). *The Theory of Economic Growth*. London: George Allen and Unwin.

Lindenberg, M., and B. Crosby (1981). *Managing Development: The Political Dimension*. West Hartford, CT: Kumarian Press.

Lipton, M. (1977). *Why Poor People Stay Poor: Urban Bias in World Development*. Cambridge, MA: Harvard University Press.

Loewenberg, G., and S. C. Patterson (1979). *Comparing Legislatures*. Boston: Little, Brown.

Maas, A. (1959). *Area and Power*. Glencoe, IL: Free Press.

Maddick, H. (1963). *Democracy, Decentralization and Development*. Bombay: Asia Publishing House.

Mansbridge, J. (1990). The rise and fall of self-interest in the explanation of political life. In J. Mansbridge, ed. *Beyond Self-Interest*. Chicago: University of Chicago Press.

Matheson, R. (1978). *People Development in Developing Countries*. New York: John Wiley and Sons.

Mawhood, P., ed. (1983). *Local Government in the Third World: The Experience of Tropical Africa*. New York: Wiley.

Mazmanian, D., and P. Sabatier (1983). *Implementation and Public Policy*. Chicago: Scott-Foresman.

Migdal, J. S. (1988). *Strong Societies and Weak States*. Princeton, NJ: Princeton University Press.

Mintzberg, H. (1973). *The Nature of Managerial Work*. New York: Harper & Row.

Montgomery, J. D. (1962). *The Politics of Foreign Aid*. New York: Frederick A. Praeger Publisher.

———— (1963). Public interest in the ideologies of development. In C. J. Friedrich, ed. *Public interest. Nomos V*. New York: Atherton Press.

———— (1972). Allocation of authority in land reform programs. *Administrative Science Quarterly* 17:62–75.

———— (1983). Decentralizing integrated rural development activities. In Cheema and Rondinelli (1983).

Montgomery, J. D., and W. Siffin, eds. (1966). *Aproaches to Development: Politics, Administration and Change*. New York: McGraw Hill.

Moore, R. (1989). Contracting out as privatization: A Honduran case study. *International Journal of Public Administration* 12:137–162.

Moris, J. R. (1976). The transfer of the western management tradition to the non-western public service sectors. *Philippine Journal of Public Administration* 20(4):401–27.

——— (1981). *Managing Induced Rural Development.* Bloomington: Indiana University International Development Institute.

Mosher, A. T. (1975). *Serving Agriculture as an Administrator.* New York: Agricultural Development Council.

Mosher, F. (1968). *Democracy and the Public Service.* New York: Oxford University Press.

Myrdal, G. (1957). *Economic Theory and Underdeveloped Regions.* London: G. Duckworth and Co.

——— (1968). *Asian Drama: An Inquiry into the Poverty of Nations.* New York: Pantheon Press.

Naisbett, J. (1982). *Megatrends.* New York: Warner Books.

Nellis, J. (1986). *Public Enterprises in Sub-Saharan Africa.* Washington, DC: World Bank.

——— (1988). *Contract Plans and Public Enterprise Performance.* Discussion Paper 48. Washington, DC: World Bank.

Nicholson, N., and E. Connerley (1989). The impending crisis in development administration. *International Journal of Public Administration* 12:385–425.

Nyerere, J. (1974). *Man and Development.* New York: Oxford University Press.

Olowu, D. (1988). Bureaucratic morality in Africa. *International Political Science Review* 9(3):215–30.

O'Toole, L. J. Jr. (1985). Diffusion of responsibility: An interorganizational analysis. In *Policy Implementaton.* See Hanf and Toonen (1985).

Owens, E., and R. Shaw (1972). *Development Reconsidered.* Lexington, MA: D. C. Heath and Co.

Paul, S. (1982). *Managing Development Programs: The Lessons of Success.* Boulder, CO: Westview Press.

——— (1983). *Strategic Management of Development Programs.* Geneva: International Labor Office.

Perrow, C. (1986). *Complex Organizations: A Critical Essay.* New York: Random House.

Peters, T. J., and R. H. Waterman (1984). *In Search of Excellence: Lessons from America's Best Run Companies.* New York: Warner Books.

Pinstrup-Andersen, P. (1982). *Agricultural Research and Technology in International Development.* London: Longmans.

Rahman, M. A., ed. (1984). *Grass Roots Participation and Self-Reliance: Experiences in South and South East Asia.* New Delhi: Oxford and IBH Publishing Co.

Ramanadham, V. V., ed. (1984). *Public Enterprise in the Developing World.* London: Croom Helm.

Richter, W. L., F. Burke, and J. Doig, eds. (1990). *Combatting Corruption: Encouraging Ethics.* Washington, DC: American Society for Public Administration.

Riggs, F. W. (1963). Bureaucrats and political development. In J. Lapalombara, ed. *Bureaucracy and Political Development.* Princeton, NJ: Princeton University Press.

————— (1964). *Administration in Developing Countries: The Theory of Prismatic Society.* Boston: Houghton Mifflin.

—————, ed. (1971). *Frontiers of Development Administration.* Durham, NC: Duke University Press.

Rondinelli, D. (1983). *Development Projects as Policy Experiments.* New York: Methuen.

————— (1987). *Development Administration and U. S. Foreign Aid Policy.* Boulder, CO: Lynn Reinner Publishers.

Rondinelli, D., and G. S. Cheema, eds. (1988). *Urban Services in Developing Countries.* London: Macmillans.

Rondinelli, D., J. Nellis, and G. S. Cheema (1984). *Decentralization in Developing Countries: A Review of Recent Experience.* Staff Working Paper 581. Washington, DC: World Bank.

Rostow, W. W. (1960). *The Stages of Economic Growth.* New York: Cambridge University Press.

Roth, G. (1987). *The Private Provision of Public Services in Developing Countries.* New York: Oxford University Press.

Rothschild, J. (1981). *Ethnopolitics: A Conceptual Framework.* New York: Columbia University Press.

Ruttan, V. (1982). *Agricultural Research Policy.* Minneapolis: University of Minnesota Press.

Saulniers, A. (1990). Improvement in public enterprise in Francophone Africa. In *Public Enterprise.* See Heath (1990).

Sauvant, K. P., and H. Hasenpflug (1977). *The New International Economic Order.* London: Walton House Publications.

Schaffer, B. (1969). The deadlock of development administration. In C. Leys, ed. *Politics and Change in Developing Countries: Studies in the Theory and Practice of Development.* New York: Cambridge University Press.

————— (1973). *The Administrative Factor: Papers in Organization, Politics, and Development.* London: Cass.

Schermerhorn, R. A. (1970). *Comparative Ethnic Relations: A Framework for Theory and Research.* New York: Random House.

Schumacher, E. F. (1973). *Small Is Beautiful.* London: Blond and Briggs.

Scott, J. C. (1972). *Comparative Political Corruption.* Englewood Cliffs, NJ: Prentice Hall.

Sherwood, F., and J. Pfiffner (1967). *Institutionalizing the Grass Roots in Brazil: A Study in Comparative Local Government.* San Francisco: Chandler Publishing Co.

Siffin, W. J., ed. (1957). *Toward the Comparative Study of Public Administration.* Bloomington: Indiana University Department of Government.

Silverman, J. M. (1990). *Public Sector Decentralization: Economic Policy Reform and Sector Investment Programs.* World Bank, Africa Region, Division Study Paper No. 1.

Smith, B. C. (1967). *Field Administration.* London: Kegan and Paul.

————— (1985). *Decentralization: The Territorial Dimension of the State.* London: Allen and Unwin.

Swerdlow, I., ed. (1963). *Development Administration: Concepts and Problems.* Syracuse, NY: Syracuse University Press.

Swerdlow, I., and M. Ingle, eds. (1974). *Public Administration Training for Less Developed Countries*. Syracuse, NY: Syracuse University, The Maxwell School.

Tendler, J. (1975). *Inside Foreign Aid*. Baltimore, MD: Johns Hopkins University Press.

————— (1988). Providing credit to small firms through private voluntary organizations: UNO in Recife, Brazil. In *Urban Services*. See Rondinelli and Cheema (1988).

United Nations. Center for Regional Development (1988). *Information Systems for Government and Business: Trends, Issues, Challenges*. Nagoya, Japan: Author.

—————. Department of Economic and Social Affairs (1975). *Development Administration: Current Approaches and Trends in Public Administration for National Development*. New York: Author.

—————. Department of International Economic and Social Affairs (1978). *Strengthening Public Administration and Finance for Development in the 1980s: Issues and Approaches*. New York: Author.

Uphoff, N. (1986a). *Improving International Irrigation Management with Farmer Participation: Getting the Process Right*. Boulder, CO: Westview Press.

————— (1986b). *Local Institutional Development*. West Hartford, CT: Kumarian Press.

Verspoor, A. (1988). *Pathways to Change: Improving the Quality of Education in Developing Countries*. Washington, DC: World Bank, Education and Training Department.

Vickers, G. (1973). *Making Institutions Work*. New York: John Wiley and Sons.

Wade, R. (1990). *Governing the Market: Economic Theory and the Role of Government in East Asian Industrialization*. Princeton, NJ: Princeton University Press.

Waldo, D., ed. (1970). *Temporal Dimensions of Development Administration*. Durham, NC: Duke University Press.

Wanasinghe, H. S. (1979). Role of peasant organizations in rural development. In *Approaches to Rural Development*. See Inayatulla (1979).

Waterston, A. (1965). *Development Planning: Lessons of Experience*. Baltimore, MD: Johns Hopkins University Press.

Weber, M. (1947). The essentials of bureaucratic organization: An ideal-type construction. In T. Parsons, ed. *The Theory of Social and Economic Organization*. London: Oxford University Press.

Weidner, E. W. (1964). *Technical Assistance in Public Administration Overseas: The Case for Development Administration*. Chicago: Public Administration Service.

White, L. G. (1989). Public management in a pluralistic arena. *Public Administration Review* 49(6):522–32.

————— (1990). *Implementing Policy Reforms in LDCs: A Strategy for Designing and Effecting Change*. Boulder, CO: Lynn Reinner Publishers.

Whyte, W. F., and D. Boynton, eds. (1983). *Higher Yielding Human Systems for Agriculture*. Ithaca, NY: Cornell University Press.

World Bank (1987). *World Development Report*. New York: Oxford University Press.

Wright, D. S. (1978). *Understanding Intergovernmental Relations*. North Scituate, MA: Duxbury Press.

Wunsch, J. S., and D. Olowu (1990). *The Failure of the Centralized State: Institutions and Self-Governance in Africa*. Boulder, CO: Westview Press.

Young, C. (1976). *The Politics of Cultural Pluralism*. Madison: University of Wisconsin Press.

Index

Accountability: of development managers, 77, 156–58; information flow and, 60; political pressures and, 67–69; to local publics, 104; of voluntary associations, 106
Ad hoc working parties, 87–88
Administrative deconcentration, 49–52
African businesses, 143
African parastatals, 99
Agricultural cooperatives (*see also* Farmers' associations), 103, 120–21
Agricultural departments, 77
Agriculture: bureaucratic social marketing in, 61; service networks in, 119, 125; state management of, 18
AIDS epidemic, 78
All-India Administrative Service, 47
American Society for Public Administration, 23
Arbitrariness, 69
Audits, 70
Authoritarian societies, 65, 67
Autonomy: of central governments, 35–37; of foreign donor projects, 138; of voluntary organizations, 104–5

Balance of power, 139
Banking, 117

Bargaining *see* Negotiation
Bilateral donors, 82
Bribery *see* Corruption
Buchanan, James, 148
Budgets *see* Financial management
Bureaucracies: abuses in, 69–71; contingency theory on, 71–73; control of, 137; ethics of, 148, 150; foreign donors and, 84; incongruence among, 85–88; interagency cooperation among, 74–90; interdepartmental interdependency in, 78–80, 88–90; local needs and, 108; nature of, 31–33; organizational principles in, 76–77; participatory management in, 64–66; performance improvement of, 47–48; pluralism in, 33–35, 36, 48, 79, 113; political pressures on, 67–69; program management and, 40–73; public interest and, 42–43; recruitment to, 43–45; remuneration of, 150; roles of, 40–42; service networks and, 126, 131; social marketing by, 60–61; structural complexity in, 76–78; structural reform of, 49–56; vertical interdependency in, 80–82; work organization in, 54–55; working conditions in, 63–64
Business schools, 100

169

ABOUT THE AUTHOR

Milton J. Esman is the John S. Knight Professor of International Studies, Emeritus, at Cornell University in Ithaca, New York. He has been a participant, observer, teacher, analyst, and commentator on international development for nearly four decades. A founder of the landmark Development Administration Group in the late 1950s, he also organized and served as first research director of the Inter-University Research Program in Institution Building in the 1960s.

In 1989 he was honored by the American Society for Public Administration with the Fred Riggs Award for Distinguished Contributions to International, Comparative, or Development Administration. He has consulted with all the major international organizations and foundations associated with Third World development and has published extensively on development administration, rural development, foreign assistance, and the politics of ethnic pluralism.

His three offspring having long since sought their fortunes in the world, Professor Esman continues to live in Ithaca with Janice, his wife, and Aneurin Chochom, their corgi. In summer he tends his roses; in winter he clears the abundant snow from the driveway; and in spring and autumn he teaches, writes, and visits his grandchildren.

Other important books from KUMARIAN PRESS:

Democratizing Development
The Role of Voluntary Organizations
JOHN CLARK

A Dragon's Progress
Development Administration in Korea
EDITORS: GERALD E. CAIDEN AND BUN WOONG KIM

Getting to the 21st Century
Voluntary Action and the Global Agenda
DAVID C. KORTEN

La gestion efficace des projets de développement
Un guide à l'exécution et l'évaluation
deuxième édition
DERICK W. BRINKERHOFF ET JANET C. TUTHILL

Managing Organizations in Developing Countries
An Operational and Strategic Approach
MOSES N. KIGGUNDU

Promises Not Kept
The Betrayal of Social Change in the Third World
JOHN ISBISTER

The Water Sellers
A Cooperative Venture by the Rural Poor
GEOFFREY D. WOOD AND RICHARD PALMER-JONES WITH
M. A. S. MANDAL, Q. F. AHMED, S. C. DUTTA

❖   ❖   ❖

For a complete catalog of
KUMARIAN PRESS titles, please call or write:

KUMARIAN PRESS, INC.
630 Oakwood Ave., Suite 119
West Hartford, CT 06110-1529 USA

tel (203) 953-0214 • fax (203) 953-8579